T0146594

CLIMBING LIFE'S ETERNAL LADDER

Wayne MacPherson

BALBOA
PRESS

A DIVISION OF HAY HOUSE

Balboa Press books may be ordered through booksellers or by contacting:

Balboa Press
A Division of Hay House
1663 Liberty Drive
Bloomington, IN 47403
www.balboapress.com
1 (877) 407-4847

Because of the dynamic nature of the Internet, any web addresses or links contained in this book may have changed since publication and may no longer be valid. The views expressed in this work are solely those of the author and do not necessarily reflect the views of the publisher, and the publisher hereby disclaims any responsibility for them.

The author of this book does not dispense medical advice or prescribe the use of any technique as a form of treatment for physical, emotional, or medical problems without the advice of a physician, either directly or indirectly. The intent of the author is only to offer information of a general nature to help you in your quest for emotional and spiritual well-being. In the event you use any of the information in this book for yourself, which is your constitutional right, the author and the publisher assume no responsibility for your actions.

Any people depicted in stock imagery provided by Thinkstock are models, and such images are being used for illustrative purposes only. Certain stock imagery © Thinkstock.

Print information available on the last page.

ISBN: 978-1-5043-6799-8 (sc)
ISBN: 978-1-5043-6801-8 (hc)
ISBN: 978-1-5043-6800-1 (e)

Library of Congress Control Number: 2016916837

Balboa Press rev. date: 10/29/2016

"A very pleasantly and lovingly written book, and all triggered by its contents will be drawn to look a bit higher up life's eternal ladder"

-Jelka Samsom, PhD,MA,PGCE

"This is a book about a love affair with life. It may well be the book you keep on your nightstand as every page is filled with nuggets that will change your perspective about the life you are living"

-Carl Bozeman, author of Amazon Best Seller- *On Being God – Beyond your Life's Purpose; Are You Listening? Addressing The Divine Within; On Human Being – Loving and Living Without Purpose;* and *Shaman*

"Wayne's book is a very like-able and inspiring read, containing some very good ideas as to how to make one's path to awakening that much smoother. Enjoyable and thought provoking"

- Steven Dean, author of *Truth Connections – An Understanding Of A Course Of Miracles*

"Whether you are just starting out on a spiritual journey, or have already found your path-you will find Climbing Life's Eternal Ladder an excellent travelling companion! A highly recommended read- for as we climb the ladder to Oneness, Wayne's book will help you scale those rungs!"

-Jane Rowley, Literary Proof Reader

CONTENTS

Dedicated lovingly to my wife Lisa and my daughters Ashley and Alyssa- and to what we have experienced together in our journey thus far. You are my greatest teachers- thank you, and love you always!

ACKNOWLEDGEMENTS

My greatest thanks need to be placed into the hands of my Source, the One who has changed my understanding and awareness. You are forever in my heart and soul.

And of course, much appreciation, love, and thanks to my immediate family- my parents Wayne and Georgina MacPherson, and my sister and brother-in-law Wendy and Rob Davies, and niece Carly. Thanks for always guiding and believing in me. To all my extended family- a heartfelt thanks as well, for accepting me in all the trials and tribulations experienced.

To my wife Lisa's family- Jack and Marie Vanderlaan, Leanne Vanderlaan and Mitch Lapointe and their daughter Allenah, Jim and Laura Cassan and their children Jake, Reagan, and Liam. You have always demonstrated the importance of family, and for this I am forever grateful.

To my spiritual friend and mentor Pam Beck. I thank you for all our conversations, and for you helping me to remember my Divine heritage. Also, special thanks to Greg Vance and Tom Burns, who shone their light toward me, to help me discover my own.

Last, but definitely not least- I would like to thank my life long- friends who have been with me through thick and thin from our days as young kids. We experienced a great deal together, and man- we had some great times! Forever thanks to Terry West, Kevin Guhl, Mike Falusi, Mike Wesny, and Peter Dominic. Everything we have done and experienced together has shaped and molded us, and I thank you all for your influence!

PREFACE

Throughout our past, present, and future—three simple words we relate to as time—we human beings have moved and will move through many realms of trials and tribulations, which we ultimately call *experience*. Each of us flows into and out of different experiences throughout our lives, throughout eternity, and with each experience, we ultimately discover who we really are.

As I have no formal education in history, philosophy, or the like, it has been my own experiences and the experiences of others I have met on the path that have instilled the strength, hope, and belief to write this book. Much of the content stems from poetry and other short writings, ideas, and simple quotations that have come through me at different points in my journey of life thus far. Of course, there have been many other outside influences that have inspired my thoughts, beliefs, understanding, and awareness, such as great songs, books, and art, written, performed, or created by others revealing their own life experiences. I believe we all pick up bits and pieces along our journey to help us further understand ourselves, and thus each other. No matter what the experience—deemed either good or bad, positive or negative, or right or wrong—they all ultimately aid us on our path to self-knowledge, a path that we all simultaneously travel down today, tomorrow, and from the beginning of time as we know it. My only request to anyone who picks up and reads this book is to keep an open mind. In reality, a key component to all of our true recognition is keeping an open mind by allowing the flow of others thoughts and words, and our own experiences- to be truly absorbed into our being. With the continual, conscious effort toward this, we develop a sense of understanding that anything is possible- as everyone and everything is constantly, continually changing. Having a belief that anything is possible, in many cases is extremely difficult, as collectively, we have been taught and conditioned on the ways of the world. At one point in time, the world was believed to have been flat. We all know how that turned out! Most of society tends to rely on scientific, fact based knowledge- and it is this which we must transcend, by keeping an open mind, to understand our true reality!

We as human beings typically walk along life's path judging, and forming ideas of our thoughts, words and actions, but more so, the thoughts, words, and actions of others we come into contact with throughout our lives. This includes those close to us whom we have continual interaction, people we may have contact with only on very few occasions, or even a singular occasion. In our typical life experiences, or what we would call our realities, thoughts inspire ideas, ideas form opinions, opinions form beliefs, and beliefs become our mental positions. This subconsciously reinforces our differences and ultimately our separation.

I determinedly believe that breaking through the walls of

separation is our key to infinite happiness—one might call a state of heaven or better yet "*estate of heaven*"! We are not what we think; we are more than we could ever imagine, and we are all awakening to the beauty and wonder of Unconditional love, one experience at a time! Knowing within that there is an infinite force that has been with us from the beginning of time as we know it and will always remain, we can rest assured our hands and feet are lovingly grounded upon the rungs of life's eternal ladder. Let us all help one another to the top, where the sky is not the limit!

INTRODUCTION

At or about the age of 30 my conscious journey with the unknown, my journey toward self-discovery, began to unfold and come more to the forefront of my life than it had been previously. Until this time, I moved along life's path, trying to conform to what I was supposed to—you know, going to school, being a "good" person, meeting a woman, getting married, and so on. I had made many mistakes in life to this point and many times fell short of "earthly" expectations. I felt disappointed in myself and ashamed for letting down the ones I loved in my life. With the experiences to this point in my life, my realization unfolded to this:

"No one should think in their minds, or believe in their hearts that they are above, or below anyone else – even though we are all on different rungs of Life's eternal ladder"

What did this instil? What did this firmly plant in the soil of my consciousness? Or realistically, what did this affirm that I already knew at a core level, that is already known to all of us in an omniscient manner? Simply put, a firm belief that no matter what may appear in our reality—the disheartening vision of someone starving for food and without adequate clothing, or the envy-evoking vision of another with all the comforts and luxuries known to humankind—we are all one and the same and blessed with Eternal, Universal love. One may call this the love of God, the love of the Universe, the love of Source, or anything else one may choose. Ultimately a loving and caring entity revealed to all of us as the layers of illusion fall by the wayside, through each and every experience.

This revelation was really only the beginning, and as I continued down life's path, doing for the most part what society would consider all the right things (being happily married, raising two beautiful girls, working at a steady job), the layers of illusion continued to cover and cloud over the true Self. Through many trials and tribulations, life experience, and reading and listening to others life experience, the layers of illusion have continued to shed, and given me a small glimpse into the window of the true Self.

And what of these layers of illusion? These layers consist of what we all deem important, unimportant, true or false, and right or wrong. They form our ideas of what we should be like, what our children should be like, or what any of our brothers and sisters or anyone else near or far should be like. These layers surround all of us, thus creating our individual and collective realities and ultimately our ego, the ever-bewildering part of the mind that persistently denies reality. Houdini and other world-renowned magicians cannot compare in the least to the greatest magician ever known to humankind, the ultimate creator of illusion—our minds, our egos!

The ego is the perfect obstruction to the truth, which is within us all, and ultimately forms our beliefs that differences in skin colour, language, socioeconomic status, or anything else we may perceive make us different from one another. Sometimes we feel more than or better than, and sometimes we feel less than or worse than; and often with a plethora of feelings in between. In every waking day, we experience these feelings sometimes consciously but a great majority of the time unconsciously, and they create an ever-changing view of ourselves and others around us. The result of these feelings ultimately reinforces our perceived separation, our individuality, and our opinions of ourselves, others, and the world around us, both on an individual and collective basis.

The individual ego resides in every living human being and reflects our feelings of ourselves at any given point in time, throughout our lifetime. It convinces us of our superiority or inferiority, our beauty or lack thereof, our belief in ourselves, or once again, lack thereof. With each new day, with each turn of the page of life, this incessant obstacle continually sways or supports our opinion of ourselves, and ultimately our opinion of others and the world we live in. It holds us captive within the confines of our thoughts and perpetually shackles us *to ourselves*!

How often do we experience ourselves or know of others in our circle of life who can be on top of the world after finding new love, landing the perfect job, or winning an all-important sports event? Feelings of happiness and elation result, and the world seems like a mighty fine place in this precise space and time. We are fully engaged with positive feelings in times such as these, feeling good about ourselves and for the most part, about the world around us, the world we live in. These experiences can be of any duration, from a few fleeting moments to days, weeks, and sometimes even years, depending on the situation or the intensity of the experience. Oh, how wonderful life would be if these experiences and ultimately the effect on the ego could go on forever! But as life continually unfolds, new situations, challenges, and experiences overcome our moments of glory and ultimately cast the little voice that resides in us all back upon the realm of comparison.

Now, let's look at the contrasting spectrum of the ego, at a time when one experiences feeling really low, when the world does not look so rosy, such as with the loss of a job, the end of an intimate relationship, or a loss in a sporting event. These events or experiences can also be of different duration but ultimately fuel feelings of inadequacy, sorrow, depression, and the like—our world and the world around us is not such a pleasant place to be in this space and time. These negative, hurtful feelings in many cases turn inward, and incessant images of failure, defeat, or lack in one form or another overcome our thoughts. In most cases, these low times cast us upon the realm of comparison as well, and typically convince us that we are inferior to or less than others we observe to have more, be happier than we are, and so on.

Ultimately these perpetual experiences, which the ego labels as "good" or "bad," create an image of who we think we are—the respected doctor, the adventurous free spirit, the hard-nosed criminal, or the hard-working average Joe. Subconsciously, the stage of life becomes set as we come into adulthood, as we have fallen and remain asleep! Our thoughts, actions, and lives revolve around protecting our self-image, typically through subconscious comparison and self-evaluation. We ultimately become our thoughts! There are incredible amounts of time and energy invested in this egoic phenomenon that ultimately consumes our thoughts, our minds. We become our thoughts, our thoughts become our identity, and the ego claims victory over our true Self, our true Being. Until we can break this subconscious pattern, we can never really discover who we are. We will explore this in greater depth later.

Now collectively, the ego contributes immensely to the state of our communities, countries, and the world far and wide. It is the most powerful unseen force on earth as we know it. It has reared its ugly head in the past and continues to do so in each day and age. When the thoughts, ideas, and beliefs of individuals in positions of authority, power, and the like begin to amalgamate and build, the results evolve to form communities, businesses, corporations, religions, cults, governments, and the like. I guess we can therefore say that the collective ego causes multiple vision- but ultimately multiple illusion!

Multiple vision? Multiple illusion? With any collective point of view, belief, or in many cases way of life, the affirmations build collectively, which can ultimately increase the vision and illusion on an individual basis. This, in turn, again adds to the collective illusion. We can relate this evolution somewhat to the creation of a tidal wave. As the wave progresses through its maturity toward shore, it builds and builds, with the accumulation of each and every water molecule joining its evolving force. Unfortunately, much like a tidal wave, the collective illusion builds to a point that can and does have extremely detrimental effects. Today happens to be Good Friday, one of, if not the most, relevant examples of the collective ego known to modern humans—the day that Christ was nailed to the cross.

The collective ego manifests itself everywhere, in every civilization, and ultimately its root cause revolves around fear—not enough power, not enough food, not enough freedom to express the beliefs of a country or a culture. People have gone and will go to any lengths to build and protect the collective ego—from governments to radical militant groups to corporate boardrooms. On behalf of the collective ego, individuals will lie, steal, cheat, abuse, and kill in the name of the cause. The ultimate goal is to protect the cause, protect the people, protect the company, or whatever the powers that be deem important, deem crucial for survival.

Genesis, one of my all-time favourite progressive rock bands, spelled out the collective insanity, fighting for its cause, in their song "Time Table." In the verse outlined here, ideas, opinions and mental positions saw men and their collective groups fight for their beliefs through lance and sword. The chorus outlines the collective position of each race deeming themselves to be of utmost caliber and position on the perpetual realm of all time and space. This group of guys had insight and wisdom at such a young age, as this song was written when they were in their early twenties.

Why, why can we never be sure till we die

Or have killed for an answer

Why, why do we suffer each race to believe

That no race has been grander

It seems because through time and space

Though names may change each face retains the mask it wore. [1]

One of the most prominent forms of the collective ego, the collective illusion, is the bodies ruling vast groups of people or countries. Any ruling body, in most cases known as a government, falls into this collective illusion. Millions of lives have been lost to fight to gain rights, protect rights, get more, keep more, gain happiness, keep happiness, and so on. Fear drives each and every one of these collective bodies and convinces its members on a continual basis that it is only in their best interest that it acts as it does, that the insane and inhumane actions are necessary to safeguard the cause.

Substantial amounts of time, resources, and money have been and continue to be invested in the protection of these bodies. The common objective centres on improving or maintaining the bodies' current state, their known state, and ultimately providing themselves their definition of happiness and fulfilment. But more so, it is the realm of the unknown that drives these illusory bodies. What is unknown manifests itself in the form of fear and propels these bodies

---

[1] Written by Anthony Banks, Michael Rutherford, Peter Gabriel, Phil Collins, Steven Hackett • Copyright © Sony/ATV Music Publishing LLC

to focus and prepare for the future, the threat of attack, the threat of nature, the threat of anything unknown!

In a lot of cases, this concern and preparation can be of benefit for its members, in providing a more stable living environment. Let's look at the development in weather forecasting. This evolution has allowed early prediction and preparation for severe weather and thus protected and saved human lives. In cases such as these, devastation has been and will continue to be better managed, but it is not these collective advancements or causes that I speak of; it is those in nature that manifest potential or actual harm. In every corner of the earth, billions are spent annually on weapons of defence to maintain or increase their position in the great pecking order. This collective insanity has gone on and will continue to go on as long as powers at the helm maintain their dream and, realistically, our nightmare.

Now, we can relate the collective ego to any other group or organization as well, but again, it all reverts back to fear—fear of loss, fear of failure, fear of takeover. In this day and age, a prominent theme in the business world is kill or be killed—not in the literal sense, but in a fashion that displays companies and corporations deriving business strategies that will be conducive to their perceived survival. What this typically entails is mandatory growth, growth to better establish financial position and ultimately continuity in the business organization itself. Of course the intent in most cases is noble— continued employment and source of income for the employees, return on investment for shareholders or owners, and contribution to communities and other charitable causes. But at what price?

Typically, when any company or corporation purchases or takes over another, someone has to lose. Companies do not maintain the same levels of staffing when they amalgamate or consume one another. Redundancies arise, and staff are put by the wayside in the name of corporate advancement, corporate security, and corporate bottom line. Fear subconsciously fuels the continuity of this illusion, as the powers that be rarely concede "enough is enough." Evidence of this business evolution is as plain as the nose on our face. How many small, independent businesses have fallen and continue to fall off the face of the earth?

Another prominent factor in business strategies is geographical change for business continuity and financial position. This has been and continues to be demonstrated on a regular basis. We have seen many companies and corporations leave their area or country for better sources of raw material, lower wages, and financial incentives from governments, to name a few motivating factors. And again, it's all in the name of financial strategy, financial success, and ultimately the company's survival—or at least this is what the company tells itself, its employees, and the community it operates within. But again, it reverts back to the collective ego, the collective illusion that more is needed to solidify the entity's existence. In North America, we have seen companies leave Canada and go south of the border to the United States, and then when wages or other financial factors arise there, the next stop is Mexico or other areas of the world. The collective ego is again at work, continually creating upheaval in its core employees' existences, continually looking for its next phase of growth and prosperity.

We can also realize the devastating impact of the collective ego in religious bodies as well. Any newspaper article or news cast will attest to the continued insanity, the unremitting strife in the Middle East, where lives are lost daily in the name of religion, in the name of each collective ego's idea of achieving its religious pursuits, its religious rights. These are blatant examples of the collective egoic insanity, but it is just as deeply rooted in many long-standing passive religious factions as well, which instil one way and one way only to achieving God's grace, eternal life, and passage to their illusory heaven. Many of these collective groups profess only those ensuing their regime will enter the pearly gates and that all others will ultimately burn in hell. Again, it is an obvious example of division, separation, and ultimately illusion. Not until these collective bodies profess unity among all living beings, will any degree of healing enter their collective consciousness. Currently they are and will continue to be trapped in collective insanity, so to speak.

These are some of the many facets of the collective ego at large, and they ultimately create an ever-increasing spiritual trap for many walking the face of the earth today, as power and purpose do ultimately grow in numbers. We need, and we will experience radical shifts in the perception of men and women at the helms of these collective egos, to where fear begins to dissipate and a new understanding emerges and takes precedence over our old ways of thinking. One of my favourite Canadian progressive rock bands, Rush, expressed this in an exceptional fashion in one line of their song, "Closer to the Heart":

"And the men who hold high places, must be the ones to start to mold a new reality, closer to the heart." [2]

Closer to the heart—the place in which we know love and our intimate reliance upon one another—near and far! The ladder of life takes us all one step closer to this ultimate reality.

So, what of this eternal ladder? What of our opinions of ourselves and all those around us? When we firmly establish that all of us, every last person and soul among our universe, is upon the eternal ladder, miraculous things begin to appear. Well, they really don't appear; they are understood in our awareness, as they have been constant from the beginning of time as we know it. We begin to see coincidences in a different light and begin to see the beauty and wonder in the world as we know it, even in the face of poverty, injustice, and perceived separation. We begin to understand that we are an extraordinarily special soul- but not any more so than any other soul, living or dead. We come to a realization that we need each other to become One, as we are One. With this realization, the layers of illusion begin to fall away, moving us from both our dreams and nightmares- to a new Reality.

And what of the rungs on the eternal ladder? As eternal beings, we all evolve and grow in our awareness of the miraculous beating heart

[2] From the 1977 album- "A farewell To Kings" music: Alex Lifeson, Geddy Lee; lyrics: Neil Peart, Peter Talbot

of our universe. With each increment of awareness, we grow in love, compassion, and understanding for all of creation- and ultimately our Creator. We are all in this together and continually move from rung to rung as both perceived sinner and saint, on the eternal ladder of life. It is only by providing a loving, helping hand and attitude to those around us- that we help those around us to begin to recognize the light and love that exists at their core as well. With each and every new increment of awareness, with each and every new migration toward light, our world, our universe continually transcends from perceived separation to loving unity of everything and everyone.

There are so many mysteries surrounding our human nature, and even though we continue to advance intellectually and technologically, we cannot seem to solve our lack of harmony. Harmony within families and countries, and throughout the entire world continues to elude us, as we subconsciously resist looking at our own rung on the ladder of life, individually and collectively. With perfectly good intent to do right by ourselves, our families, and our communities, we still experience conflict and unrest. And why? For the most part, we subconsciously ignore the miraculous energy that surrounds and bonds everything and all of us in the material world.

These mysteries rear their ugly heads on a daily basis, and can evolve from a simple conversation with a friend or loved one. We can be involved in any conversation at any time, with the full intent to peacefully talk over or discuss just about anything, and at any given time, our thoughts, feelings, and subsequent words and actions can take a turn for the worse. And typically, the turn is a result of our disagreement or difference of opinion as to the content of the interaction. Unfortunately, in many cases, these individual experiences tend to cling to us internally and build to a point of crisis. Yes, in many cases, they do get resolved on the surface, but internally they lay subconsciously dormant. In time, these relationships can deteriorate to varying degrees of partial to total separation.

Through the ongoing accumulation of these incidences or experiences, there is a decline in the quality of the relationship, and interaction is strained or limited. At this point, spending time together or talking deteriorates and breaks down, and the simple joy of a relationship that once was begins to lose its lustre. Communicating oftentimes becomes an emotionally strenuous chore, and the evolution of the relationship shifts to varying degrees of separation. Yes, these relationships may continue to exist, but ultimately we are here on earth to live, not simply exist. We begin to feel like the wind has been taken out of our sails. If our sails can no longer support any wind whatsoever, total separation is inevitable.

The same deterioration in any collective relationship happens much in the same way, when communication and trust decline, and the bonds that once existed eventually experience breakdown. Emotional and mental positions become established, one experience or event at a time. Again, this can lead to varying degrees of partial to full separation. We see this on a regular basis with political parties, communities, business allies, and countries. Once strong, cohesive, and beneficial collective relationships often disintegrate, and ultimately both sides of the coin suffer, whether they want to believe or admit it or not. Anytime separation to any degree takes place, it reinforces fear deep within, and that fear thus manifests in further actions or behaviours in a cyclical manner.

This miraculous energy mentioned earlier is our only salvation and solution to the disharmony we all experience to varying degrees within our lives, within our existence. This energy is not subject to our five senses- but ultimately is our most important sense and our most important guidance in understanding the mysteries of our own nature, our human nature, and the nature of our entire universe. This energy, this force, is much like a magnetic field that exists but cannot be seen. We can easily substantiate the existence of a magnetic field by simply putting a magnet under a piece of paper, and then sprinkling metal filings onto the paper. A clear, distinct pattern results, and we can visually see what cannot be see without the integration of a magnet, the piece of paper, and the metal filings. Like this known magnetic force, this miraculous energy, this miraculous force, surrounds everyone and everything in our universe. It perpetually flows into, out of, and around every known and unknown entity in existence, much like our own breath, our own heartbeat.

Upon life's eternal ladder, we experience this life force, this energy, to varying degrees. With increased awareness of this Force, our understanding toward ourselves, toward others, and toward life itself ultimately changes. It changes, it evolves, and it migrates toward light, toward love, and toward a power that reflects the unity of all- and dissipation of individuality, separation, and dualism. With a decline in this separation, we better understand ourselves and everything and everyone in our reality. This miraculous life force ultimately invades and changes our past perception of how the material world works and our position and existence within it. Understanding of the ways of the world are then subjected to a paradigm shift, a shift that radiates pure joy in living, pure joy in experiencing life itself, and the pure joy of Love.

Who in their right mind would not want to experience pure joy in life? For the most part, deep down, most people want to be happy, joyous, and free, no matter what their circumstance. But realistically this evades many for most of their lives, or their entire lives. Of course there are many throughout the world without adequate food, shelter, and other basic necessities who would be ecstatic to have their basic needs fulfilled, but what I refer to here aligns with what we all desire after our basic needs are met. Pure joy should not be confused with pleasure, as pleasure can, and is, experienced on any rung of the eternal ladder, at any given time. Pure joy or bliss, however, can only be experienced in varying degrees when one is "in tune" with our real life force, our real energy. Pure joy is really a phenomenal gift from the universe itself!

It is this joy that grows within us and radiates upon others, that ultimately moves our human species toward advancing collectively on the eternal ladder. And although we can all want this joy, although we can all seek this joy, we can only experience it when life gives us the green light, typically a bit at a time and typically through our own experiences. Ultimately, our responsibility is to ignite a spark in others to find joy upon the eternal ladder, and know deep within that we are all in this together!

In 2007 and 2008, I wrote several poems and quotations based on feelings experienced in this space and time. I had been subconsciously searching deeply for more meaning in life, and even with a great career, a loving family, and all the comforts of home, I still experienced an unknown void in my existence. The light of understanding had definitely gone up several notches, but I ultimately continued on life's path, one experience at a time. Through these experiences, which I now realize were neither good nor bad, right nor wrong, positive nor negative, I now realize I did not write these poems; they in fact have been writing me! They have paved the way and led me down the path toward my own current inner knowledge, understanding, and awareness, which continues to grow in depth, and ultimately in love toward all.

And how did they write me? How did they shape me? Well, as mentioned earlier, we can form an opinion on any given subject or situation, and that can move us toward accepting and even believing in our mental position. When I wrote these poems, quotes, and short writings, I had belief in them. Now, I know them to be the truth at the core of my being and that these writings came *through* me and were not written *by me*. Ultimately, the universal Force, our universal heart, is responsible, and I feel truly blessed to be able to share with all interested. Again, keep an open mind when experiencing this book and its writings, and stop and reflect when your heartstrings incline you to do so! I would also encourage rereading the poems that start each chapter prior to proceeding to the next.

Chapter 1

TRUTH

Truth

In the midst of all actions, all feelings and thought
There is but one thing to prevail,
The many twists and turns, a step at a time
Life's sole purpose, is this to unveil.

Removing the blanket that covers true Being
Age-long passage, from time of eternal youth,
In good times and bad, in knowing or not
What is sought-is simply the truth.

Many times afraid- of that which is real
We burrow and hide in deceit,
Consciously unaware in current presence
True knowledge, is that which we cheat.

Peeling away the many layers of illusion
Through experience, one layer at a time,
No certitude of that right or wrong
On the unequivocal, true upward climb.

Perpetual change in earthly understanding
Until the ripples of judgment subside,
This stirring moment does wait for us all
And then, the truth cannot hide.

Truth now exposed, a cleansing of apparition
We experience each moment nonaligned,
Accepting the now, the instant, the present
Is our enchanting, everlasting true find.

Truth is a single, simple word that all of us have heard from our earliest days of comprehension. From the days of our childhood, we were always told to tell the truth, that telling the truth was the right thing to do and would make us good people. Of course, this was positive, constructive direction from our parents, loved ones, teachers, and the like. In reality, it helped meld us with positive character traits and attributes in our human growth and development.

But as young children, we were continually conditioned, continually bombarded with what society considered to be the truth, what society considered to be the way of the world, what society considered to be right or wrong. This idea of truth led us to believe that when we, or others, were not acting, speaking, or directing our lives in a certain fashion, we were treading down the wrong path. "Conform to the norm" would be an appropriate description of this paradigm, and history has shown that this way of thinking has continued from generation to generation. Truths, attitudes, and behaviour pass from parent to child—with good intent in most circumstances. And, of course, the best intention directs the next generation to know the way to happiness and to being a good, upstanding member of society and a good human being. Yes, there are obvious changes in traditions from several generations long past, but the core impression of the ways of the world has remained constant, and for the most part, they have been shared with an "earthly" understanding of love.

This earthly understanding of love is experienced with those close to us, both family and friends and others in our close circle of life. Many claim they love unconditionally; many believe in their own minds they love unconditionally—but in reality, when the people they love stop conforming to direction, guidance, or the attitude of others, those who thought they loved unconditionally begin to judge them and take on other attitudes that ultimately affect their relationships. Our upset or discontent with the actions, behaviour, or attitudes of others eventually goes against the grain of the universal heart. This is the way of the world as we know it, but there is good news, great news, in fact! It is exactly this process that each and every human being needs to pass through to experience and ultimately learn to love in accord with the universal heart.

Learning the truth, learning love—this is our ultimate destiny in the game that we all know as life. And how does this happen? How does this occur for each and every one of us? Ultimately, with one interaction with another person, one new conscious thought, one experience at a time. Each and every experience does not lead us toward the truth, but it eventually carries us away from what is not true, what is not real, what is not relevant in our journey as eternal beings. In many ways, it goes against the grain of what we learned in our youth as the truth—the truth we learned to carry us through life as our predecessors displayed in their actions, thoughts, and words. It peels away the many illusions that block us from knowing real love, Universal Love. In a sense, we have to unlearn that which has established our foundation as human beings, from time of birth to our present moment.

"We continually need to unlearn, and by doing this, we learn to be"

We tread down the path of life trying to conform to the wishes and directions of those who came before us. We follow our loved ones' guidance and wisdom, typically trying to conform to societal norms and lead a good, upstanding life. These loved ones typically profess that we can do anything we set our minds to with dedication and commitment. This may include following in our families' footsteps—attending certain academic institutions or taking particular career paths, or often following our parents' dreams and aspirations for us, aspirations that we make better lives for ourselves than what they themselves experienced. Again, it's all done with good intent. But imminently, we tread off this course to varying degrees, and ultimately, we develop mental images of ourselves in accordance with our non-conformance to the expectations set before us. This process typically begins at a very young age—and our conscious and subconscious positions continuously evolve. Yes, in a lot of cases, life plays out and follows the map put forth in front of us with great precision, but if the map outlined was not in accordance with universal love, it can then repeat itself and continue to elude the truth.

So how do we migrate toward the truth by either staying on or stepping off the path in front of us? Ultimately, we go where the winds of change carry us; we each trek upon our own path one step at a time, one rung on the ladder at a time, to discover who we really are at the core of our being. There are an infinite number of paths, but all eventually lead to the same destination, the same divine Truth!

Every path has many twists and turns; there's no doubt whatsoever! We experience many, many periods in our lives of happiness, sorrow, confusion, anger, intolerance, and every other emotion known to humankind. Typically, we discover what brings us happiness, what brings us pleasure, and what brings us purpose- and repeat these experiences to return to our sense of pleasure, happiness, or purpose. This becomes our perceived truth, often the same truth that has been shared by our predecessors. It can be in our choice of employment, our pleasure in any type of activity, our lifetime partner, or a group or club we associate ourselves with. We return to our passions, day in and day out, and continually chase the feelings we initially experienced upon discovering our happiness or pleasure. Many times, our experiences pan out well with what we make a part of us, sometimes for the remainder of our lives. But all too many times, the tides of change wash in, and discontent, sorrow, and a multitude of other personal disturbances are a prominent feature of their unwanted arrival.

We see this truth in personal relationships all the time, where love flourishes and happily ever after is the reference point on the ladder of life. Physical and emotional attraction permeates the essence of the new relationship, and the lovers are lenient toward each other's undesirable characteristics or personality traits. As we have heard a thousand times and we all recognize, the relationship is in the honeymoon stage. In this day and age, "until death do us part" is falling by the wayside as separation and divorce rates steadily increase from only a few decades ago.

Of course, one can ponder the possibility of many relationships in the past that may have been severely strained- as one or both participants lived or simply existed in pain and turmoil. But the pain or strain of any relationship only makes us stronger in our known or unknown quest for the truth. As people weather the storms of adversity in a loving relationship, the waves of turmoil can and do subside, one storm at a time, and peace and happiness can result if both participants maintain their hearts' targets.

But in many circumstances in this day and age, when the honeymoon is over and leniency toward undesirable characteristics or behaviours of the significant other reaches a certain level of intolerance, relationships often dissolve. One or both participants in the relationship can no longer bear the unwanted hurt, the sense of loss of the elation once felt, or the overall decline in the state of well-being. The answer? Don't accept any more pain, discontent, or suffering, and find the elation you once felt in a new, exciting relationship! Find a new source of truth! This can occur rapidly, sometimes while the old relationship still exists to some degree.

The new relationship rapidly removes the pain and discontent of the old, and pleasure, happiness, and excitement return with a huge sigh of relief. Life resonates with a new vibrancy, and once again, the horizon appears amazingly bright! In some cases, this works out well for the remainder of the journey if other segments of the truth are coming to light. But for many, the cycle repeats itself to a point of another separation or a settling for what is. Life once again loses its lustre, and we step once again onto the plane of simple existence- and off the plane of happiness and contentment.

This cycle, the experience of a personal relationship described above, can pertain not only to intimacy but to any other personal relationship as well. This could include a friendship or a relationship in business or the workplace or with any sibling or other relative. Depending on the circumstance or type of personal relationship, separation, avoidance, or a discontented existence evolve as the result, unless one has the perseverance to move through the pain.

When we experience the decline or strain in a friendship, many times the relationship simply folds, and we move on to new friends or acquaintances to replace our loss. The wrong things may have been said, intolerable actions may have taken place, or any other occurrence that creates emotional pain may push our acceptance level to the point of no return. We feel we are no longer in the emotional position to accept the situation, and we depart with varying degrees of scarring upon our soul, depending upon the level of the relationship. So much like the intimate relationships described earlier, friendships dissolve without commitment to work through the discrepancies or issues, as in many cases, the participants feel that parting ways is the easier, softer route. Either route we take—committing to resolve or parting ways—we continue to evolve toward the next removal of the un-truth and peel back one more layer of illusion!

We have touched upon the experiences of many personal relationships, but we can experience and move through many of the same frustrations, emotions, and pain in our work and working relationships as well. In many circumstances, our workplace or place of employment demands us to remain constant, and we have to tolerate and work through the many unsettling circumstances. As we grow through adolescence into adulthood, enter intimate relationships, have children, and have to support or contribute to the family unit, picking up and leaving for bigger and better things or a better working environment is many times not an option with the resources, opportunities, training, or education we may happen to possess. We remain in undesirable situations out of sheer necessity to feed our families, pay our bills, or maintain whatever lifestyle we may have developed.

Many look upon this type of work or working experience as an inescapable trap. People experience it oftentimes as a ball-and-chain existence that perpetuates day in, day out, year after year, while those involved are ever growing in frustration, discontent, and emotional torment. There is no escape, as there are mouths to feed, bills to pay, education funds to generate, and so on. Oftentimes the individual or collective discontent strikes out verbally, physically, or in other destructive manners against "the man," the company, or the known managers or leaders of such organizations. The hard truth of discontent in our livelihood is often the result, and without a positive balance of other external activity, personal fulfilment and an overall sense of well-being continue to elude us. The truth, again, is nowhere to be found.

On the other side of the coin, many do pursue their own truth through several jobs or even several career paths. Whether an individual goes out on a limb to leave a job in hopes of something better or their education, training, or experience permit this activity, the pot of gold at the end of a new rainbow becomes the next employment experience. Oftentimes the promise of more money, better opportunities, or better working conditions lure individuals to make the move toward a new road to happiness, a new road to truth. Once again, sometimes fulfilment is a result of the changes we have made, but many times, the grass is not any greener and the search for the truth trudges on to the next pasture.

So inevitably, we pursue the truth through finding happiness, finding purpose, finding fulfilment—being a good neighbour, being a good family member, being a good employee, or being a good partner. We can follow the many paths that our predecessors instructed us to take in the quest for happiness and in the quest for the truth, but an emptiness often remains. We still do not know who we are, and we still experience frustration, confusion, and judgment with ourselves and others within and outside our circle of life. We still experience a hole in our hearts to one degree or another.

It is only when we realize we must dispel our expectations, dispel judgment of our circumstances, and dispel judgment of ourselves and others that we can really begin to know the truth. And as guidance by our predecessors outlined what was right or wrong and good or bad, this leads us to a rung on the ladder of utmost confusion. How can all those before us be so certain, so steadfast in their convictions of the ways of the world, and we as individuals now question all we have learned and absorbed from youth? How do we move forward, seeing life with a different set of eyes? At this point of our journey, on this rung of the ladder, we begin to rely on the Unseen energy, the divine guidance around and within, as our level of awareness now permits.

We can begin to really comprehend and appreciate the multitude of circumstances, experiences, and outcomes for ourselves and others around us to be of divine purpose and not a simple roll of the dice. We now know that at the core of our being there is a perfect order, and we all play an intricate part each and every moment! This is when we begin to know the truth; this is when we do begin to see the world through a different set of eyes! Our new sense of being allows us to understand the multitude of paths to the truth for ourselves and all others and dispels the notion of right and wrong, good and bad, black and white. Another progressive rock band that I have grown to love is the Moody Blues. In their song "Late Lament," they describe this so well, as follows:

> **Cold-hearted orb that rules the night,**
> **Remove the colours from our sight,**
> **For red is grey-yellow-white,**
> **But we decide which is right—**
> **And which is an illusion.** [3]

No good or bad, right or wrong, black or white? Impossible, in the eyes of the material world as we know it. We have developed systems and been conditioned in every area of life to evaluate, study, grade, judge, categorize, and so on. These systems tell us what is right or wrong, according to the collective body at the helm, the powers that be. Systems created out of necessity for justice and order that ultimately reinforce our separation and individuality. It is only when we experience the universal energy at the core of our being that the

---

[3]   From the album- Days of Future Passed- The Moody Blues; lyrics- Graeme Edge

labels of judgment begin to fall by the wayside and the miracle of the eternal ladder is recognized.

And just how do we arrive at this point of recognition, this point of awareness? Only when the ever-so-stubborn shell of the ego is compromised and cracked wide open do we get a glance at who we really are. We are now aware that we are not our incessant thoughts; we are not a small, singular entity walking the face of the earth, scratching out a meagre existence. We are in fact a crucial segment of the entire universe, the entire cosmos, and we are loved beyond our wildest dreams! Without each and every one of us, life as it is known would not exist. This is the key to our entire existence, the rung of the ladder that holds our eyes wide open to the truth. This is the key to our new reality—heaven on earth! Heaven on earth is the point in time when we comprehend our innermost self to be so much more than we could have ever imagined, not in the light of the ego, but in the light of Love!

We have a new awareness of ourselves and all those around us, an awareness that floods us with divine equality and divine unity. Upon arrival on this rung of the ladder, we awaken to realize life as we know it is in a perfect state, for us and the entire universe. It is now, always has been, and will continue to be throughout time as we know it. With this recognition, with this awareness, we now understand and know Unconditional Love at our core and are forever grateful for the unseen energy coursing our being, coursing our universe!

So one can most certainly ask how our past and current existence can be in a perfect state. We have war, famine, poverty, injustice, prejudice, and every other state of oppression. People die in every part of the world every minute of the day at the hand of some injustice or atrocity. We read the paper or watch the news and see day in and day out the troubles, horrors, and nightmares of the world we live in. Of course, we have sympathy, empathy, and loving thoughts for the innocent victims upon our screen. And on the other side of the coin, we have anger, hate, and other ill thoughts and attitudes toward the perpetrators of the horrendous acts committed. It is indeed a very hard pill to swallow—to say, feel, or know that things are in perfect order.

The truth we see, the truth we experience through the eyes of the world as we know it, cries out for alleviation of all the wrongdoings and screams for justice for all those inflicting the pain, the suffering, the horrendous atrocities. In reality, there is only one way to fathom any of these worldly truths, one way to know all is perfect in this imperfect world. This one way, this one truth, is knowing the love of our Creator and knowing that all that we see is not in vain, is not without reason, is not without divine purpose. It is easy to say but most times impossible to comprehend at our core; however, it essential in our earthly understanding, essential in our growth and progression upon the ladder. With dysfunction all around us in one way, shape, or form, it is a very, very hard pill to swallow indeed.

The dysfunction we see in the world around us is often hard to comprehend, hard to take, hard to accept. It's an even greater challenge—perhaps our greatest—when dysfunction occurs in our own corner of the world, the corner of the world that really affects us the most. This can include direct family, close friends, neighbours, and the like. My own corner of the world was tossed about very recently within my own family, with my own children, and it is in times such as these that our understanding is really put to the test and we are really challenged to know and remember the truth. We can know the ladder of life very intimately, but we can still get lost in the heat of the moment when experiences take a turn away from light, away from love. It hurts us to see our loved ones slip into and experience darkness, but again, at our core, we need always remember that love does prevail.

In the poem "Truth," the core of this chapter, the last verse implies that we see things differently when we know the truth; we have a cleansing of apparition, a radical shift in our earthly understanding, a radical shift in our inner awareness. Knowing about this shift or having a belief in or true desire to experience this shift, we can begin to let the thoughts of judgment within our minds slow down and ultimately subside. We can know that in reality, we know not what is good, bad, right, or wrong for ourselves or anyone else for that matter, and judging our thoughts only holds us prisoner in the state we have come to grow into and come to know. Again, I can relate this to another one of my favourite bands' songs "Already Gone," by the Eagles. Reflect on this verse, and maybe have a listen to the song when you have the chance!

"So oftentimes it seems, we live our lives in chains, and we never even know we have the key."[4]

The *key*, again, is a simple word, but in the context of truth, it is one of the most important words we can ever learn. Our key to opening this

---

[4] From the album –On The Border by the Eagles 1974 lyrics: Jack Tempchin, Robb Strandlund

door, to experiencing an exponential paradigm shift really depends on our awareness and our ability to be fluid to life itself, to move in and out of each and every experience with no mental position, opinion, or judgment on what may or may not or what does or does not occur. With this key, we can experience a freedom beyond our wildest dreams, as with no position on any outcome, we really have absolutely nothing to lose! The ability to exist within this capacity is of course ever so complicated to comprehend as well as carry out. For the most part, the great majority of human beings walking the face of the earth have hopes, expectations, and goals with anticipated outcomes.

This can be on a large scale, such as a career path, or as simple as the anticipated pleasure of a meal one might prepare for the family or other guests. Each and every waking day, our thoughts take us in the direction of anticipated outcomes, and each and every waking day, our thoughts typically let us down at some point in our waking moments, sometimes several times. With our anticipated outcomes so many times denied, we experience various levels of unpleasant thoughts— anger, sadness, frustration, and hurt. Sure, we brush them off and get back in the saddle once again, but there is undeniably a cumulative effect that clings to our subconscious and contributes to our sense of self, our sense of well-being.

Being fluid to our everyday experiences and embracing them no matter if we look upon them as good or bad, certainly is a major stride toward the truth. As our level of light and our level of awareness increases, this will assuredly resonate within.

Chapter 2

EMBRACE

Embrace

Sun rays peek over a far distant hill,
The night's mist now beginning to rise.
Embrace the day with vigour, with thrill,
Embrace the warmth, the blue skies.

Darkness swallows the last morsel of light,
Clouds gently swept across moon.
Embrace the quiet, the stillness of night,
Embrace peaceful slumber that comes soon.

Pleasure be welcomed by both young and old,
Time engulfed in excitement and bliss.
Embrace the joy, as a mountain of gold,
Embrace, like love's first sweet kiss.

Pain does come knocking upon life's door,

It consumes the luminescence within.

Embrace the anguish, until no more,

Embrace pain, in absence of chagrin.

Miraculous the instant when child is born,

Life, giving birth unto itself,

Embrace all moments, when even weary and worn,

Embrace life, and its true unseen wealth.

Sombre the moment when life does expire,

When death befalls one of our own.

Embrace the finality, the emotions set afire,

Embrace death, one step closer to home.

In darkness or light, in pleasure or pain,

Embrace everything, being fluid to all.

Life and death, no real loss, only gain,

When we embrace our only True call.

The *Merriam-Webster* dictionary's third portion of the full definition of *embrace*, as a noun, simply states "acceptance." It seems so easy, so effortless, so welcoming to embrace, to accept all the moments in life that leave us with a sense of happiness, pleasure, warmth, and joy. These are the moments and the experiences that bring a smile to our face, put a spring in our step, and provide us with an overall sense of well-being, purpose, pride, and appreciation for life itself. These are the moments and experiences we live for, and they happen numerous times throughout our journey as a parent, a spouse or partner, a neighbour, or a team member.

The day I became aware I was going to be a parent was one like no other, until the day my children actually arrived in the world. For me, these were the most fascinating, joyous two days in my life, and they are with me as if it were yesterday. It's times such as these—our weddings, our children's arrivals, anniversaries, and other momentous occasions—that we can embrace with ease. We feel these experiences at our core, and they can most certainly be described as times of extreme happiness and elation. These times I speak of are benchmarks in our lives, which can give us a tremendous sense of joy and well-being, often for quite some time.

We can also experience pleasure in so, so many other ways, that again are very welcome and easily accepted. Memorable vacations, an enjoyable movie, a sporting event when our home team comes out on top, a completed goal in our place of employment—these events in our life can occur often, on a regular basis. With spiritual balance present on our current rung of the ladder, they can provide a healthy contribution to our overall sense of well-being. They can keep us well grounded, contribute to our ongoing motivation, and provide good reasons to lift our heads off the pillow day in and day out.

On the other side of the coin, we can and do experience many other times in our lives that we would never want to accept or embrace. These are times we are in the heart of an experience and are caught up in the heat of the moment, in the clutch of emotion, and acceptance is typically the last thing on our minds—especially in fight-or-flight situations. We often go on autopilot, adrenaline kicking and screaming, and move through the experience many times not even aware of our words, thoughts, or actions. These situations could include coming upon an automobile accident, a sudden physical altercation, or an unexpected verbal outburst by a friend or loved one, to name a few.

These types of experiences typically put us in a state of emotional turmoil, confusion, and unrest. Unpleasant events momentarily rock our world and can often throw us into state of unrest momentarily or sometimes for quite a while after the initial experience. As stated earlier, these experiences can and do typically happen often, and their cumulative effect can debilitate our overall sense of well-being. Obviously stated, some of these types of experiences cannot be avoided in our lives, such as coming upon an accident or perhaps suddenly being bitten by a dog. But in some other types of these momentary experiences, such as a verbal or physical altercation, avoidance is possible through our constant vigilance and constant desire to change our position on the eternal ladder, and thus our overall awareness.

We also experience more intense and debilitating times of unrest—the death of a loved one, the loss of a job, the breakdown in a long-term relationship. Our ability to embrace, to accept, can move in and out of us for extensive time periods and cast us upon some of the stormiest seas that life can muster up. We can find ourselves teetering between acceptance and non-acceptance for variable timeframes—sometimes minute to minute, day to day, week to week, or any combination thereof. It is these times of uncertainty, these times of emotional havoc, that can be extremely detrimental, exceedingly devastating to our overall sense of well-being. We may find some or all of our passions or interests gone by the wayside in times such as these. We can lose our zest for life and our interest in others in our circle of life and in our relationships. The continual inner turmoil of acceptance and then non-acceptance renders us unable to function to any degree of the normalcy we once experienced, for varying amounts of time.

As hard as times such as these may be, it is always in our best emotional and spiritual interest to embrace and accept these experiences as early and as whole-heartedly as possible. Again, it's easy to say but often so very hard to achieve. So what makes these unsettling, disturbing experiences acceptable, embraceable? Really, one thing and one thing only—an inner knowledge at the core of our being that there is Divine purpose to each and every experience or situation that is put in front of us, throughout our lives. This premise has been around for ages in all parts of the world. I can recall hearing from an early age the saying "There's a reason for everything"; it became a well-known phrase regarding life, and I'm sure the majority of us have heard it on more than one occasion. It is only through life's experiences and the grace of divine awareness that we really begin to take this to heart.

When we can sense the premise of Divine purpose at the core of our Being, it is then that we can begin to allow acceptance to flow into us more frequently and with less resistance. And when we embrace and accept any situation of adversity, which one would deem negative, undesirable, or unfortunate, the ongoing and residual effects subsequently diminish. We can maintain and appreciate an overall sense of peace of mind and know that there is indeed light at the end of the tunnel. We can know that things will be all right and that we are successively advancing spiritually through each and every challenge of adversity life puts forth before us.

"Adversity is but a means to an end, and thus a new beginning"

When we do flow out of any undesirable experience or time of adversity with any amount of acceptance, simultaneously a new level of awareness is instilled within us. And ultimately, it is with each and every experience we flow through that our awareness increases throughout our journey in life and we can then encounter different rungs on the ladder. When embracing and accepting those experiences that generate pain and unrest within, we can move toward understanding our true Self in a softer manner. We can move toward the truth, toward love, with a diminished sense of suffering.

We have looked at embracing experiences, both welcome and unwelcome. Let us now delve into the intricacies of our personal relationships. It is our experiences, including our experiences in our relationships, that ultimately lead us to the truth and that we need to embrace to move us along the eternal ladder. Obviously we can control some our undesirable relationships to a greater degree than we can undesirable experiences, simply by choosing to stay in them or leave them. Our greatest challenges are the relationships that are a part of us from birth—parents, siblings, children, and any other close blood relatives. These relationships, we are born into, and in many cases, it is much more difficult to just pick up and leave than in other relationships, such as friendships, working relationships, or neighbourhood acquaintances, to name a few.

In most of our experiences, it is our close, intimate relationships with our families—mainly parents, spouses, and siblings—that consume a great deal of our daily lives and generate a great deal of our emotions, thoughts, and feelings. The amount and period of time with each of these relationships is obviously influenced by the stage of life we happen to be in. It is in these relationships that we can experience the most pleasure and joy but also the most frustration, anger, and pain. It is precisely these relationships that challenge our tolerance, understanding, and ultimately our acceptance.

Many times, it is very difficult to embrace, to accept experiences or situations that arise in these relationships, and many times our experiences and interactions throw us into periods of anger, resentment, and frustration for varying periods of time and varying degrees of separation. Disagreements, arguments, callous or demeaning words, or other types of personal conflict are not uncommon in these relationships. Brothers and sisters fighting like cats and dogs, parents instilling rules with a sense of militant authority, children not fulfilling a requested or required task, and other events such as these can and do occur on a regular basis, and much like the fight-or-flight situation discussed earlier, they can be almost impossible to embrace in the heat of the moment. Our only course toward reducing some of the impact of these events is accepting and dealing with the situations in as timely a fashion as possible. Realistically, there are incidents in many family units that occur and the residual effects last for days, months, years, and even decades.

"Acceptance removes the sharp edge of the tongue, and the dull pain of the mind"

Is this right or wrong? Is this good or bad? There is no definitive answer to these questions, but they most certainly contribute to the removal of illusion for all participants involved, the illusion that exposes the truth, which we all ultimately seek. We can look upon these relationships, which many times create and maintain extremely hard feelings and ill will but also many times create and reflect a new level of awareness and love toward one another that would not have come to fruition had the situation not evolved as it had.

All of us, throughout our lives, get what we need, when we need it to assist in our growth upon the ladder and in our ever-increasing awareness. The Rolling Stones hit the nail on the head with the chorus in their song "You Can't Always Get What You Want":

> **You can't always get what you want,**
> **You can't always get what you want,**
> **You can't always get what you want—**
> **but if you try sometimes, you just might find,**
> **you get what you need.** [5]

Often in life and many, many times in our close family relationships, we don't get what we want, but we do get exactly what we need for our own evolution toward love. As mentioned earlier, these tarnished relationships can carry on and fester for substantial periods of time and often draw other family members into the underlying turbulence. There can be multitudes of interactions that are extremely difficult to embrace and accept, but when we do so, one experience at a time, the divine grace of awareness becomes our light at the end of the tunnel and our next step upon the ladder to intimately knowing a new reality.

Our close, intimate family relations can be, and in most cases are, the largest testing grounds for our emotional well-being and our ability to embrace the continual interactions within relationships. They can test our awareness, our understanding, and our patience to excessive levels no doubt! These are some of the relationships that can

---

[5] Songwriters: Keith Richards / Mick Jagger
You Can't Always Get What You Want lyrics © Abkco Music, Inc

bring our awareness to new levels on a continual basis if we commit to working through our differences and embrace the times that create upset or frustration. Without the continued effort to work through, settle, and forget the undesirable situations, we can stunt our ability to varying degrees to advance in our earthly understanding and our overall awareness.

In a lot of our relationships, with varying degrees of intimacy, we evaluate their importance and our own commitment toward them. There is nothing like having close friends to go through our lives with, to share our good and bad times with, and to mutually be there for in times of need. These types of friendships are those that are as close, and often closer in nature than some of our blood relationships. I have been extremely fortunate to still live in the area I grew up in and still be close to many lifetime friends, and the friendships developed in the very, very early stages of life. Upon the eternal ladder, these are the exact relationships that have formed and evolved for my friends' and for my own personal growth toward awareness. We have shared and been through a lot together, and I am forever grateful for all of my close friends. Thanks, guys! Did these friendships, these relationships, come easy? Absolutely not! Did they cause anger, frustration, jealousy, and other undesirable feelings and emotions? Absolutely! But did these relationships bring extreme joy, pleasure, and memories to last a lifetime? Absolutely!

Many times throughout our relationships, events or experiences took place that stirred many of these undesirable feelings, thoughts, and emotions and created strife, animosity, and ill feelings for varying durations of time. It was only through embracing and accepting these life situations and experiences, good and bad, over different periods of time that we still maintain our relationships today. My experience is no different than any other lifelong friendship that any of us encounters; these relationships have shaped and molded all of us to a great degree, whether we realize it or not.

Just this morning, I had coffee with one of my lifelong friends who works away from the area on a regular basis. We reminisced about the music we both have surrounded ourselves with over the years. Much of this music he introduced to me, and it has had a profound impact on my life. It has struck a nerve within and has most certainly led me in the direction of truth. It includes music by bands such as Genesis, King Crimson, Yes, Gentle Giant, and Rush, to name a few.

I consider myself and my friends extremely fortunate to have been born in an era that generated such deep, philosophical music and lyrics, the kind of stuff that can really touch us at the core of our being, the kind of stuff that can light the spark of eternal knowledge. Many of these artists reflect and display phenomenal awakening, and they display their appreciation for their understanding and awareness in their music. They are giving back to life what was given to them and ultimately striking a chord with those who are ready. Listen and feel this music, and truth will permeate what you already know deep within.

In the next couple of weeks, another engagement is planned to review an upcoming ATV trip with three other lifelong friends and their spouses. Last summer, the four of us experienced a four-day ATV trip in northern Ontario that was enjoyable beyond belief!

These friends and others close to me have definitely had a huge impact on who I've become. Again, in all of our lives, our close and lifelong friends play a large role on our journey upon the ladder. I would ask you now to reflect on your experiences and journeys with your long-time and close friends and the impact they have all had on your evolution and development. I'm guessing the impact has been significant!

We also encounter several other types of relationships throughout our lives, with many people flowing into and out of our lives in varying degrees of time. Perhaps we are in a field that requires us to relocate on a regular basis or work in an environment with high turnover, or we take up many types of activities that introduce us to new friends and acquaintances on a regular basis. Naturally, these types of relationships are the ones I speak of that we can turn off or on without much consideration, unlike our close, intimate family relationships or long-time friendships. But ultimately, we benefit by putting equal effort into harmony in these relationships as any of our close ties.

Yes, it appears very easy and irrelevant to vacate relationships such as these; we can simply shut down communication, stop any contact, and move on with our lives. We many times feel that relationships of this nature do not influence and impact our overall well-being if we decide that there is little value in the effort required to alleviate any differences. But this is so very far from the truth, as any unresolved disturbance within any of us has unknown, unforeseen residual effects that stir within our subconscious and eventually surface in one way, shape, or form.

Does this mean that we must maintain and experience these types of relationships indefinitely, in frustration, discontent, or anger? Absolutely not. We have the choice to associate with those whom we see fit within these types of relationships, but we need to dissolve any undesirable relationships in a manner that is in line with natural law, a manner that is hopefully peaceful to ourselves and the other individual or individuals involved. It's not always easy, but it's definitely worth the effort as opposed to simply abandoning the situation. Any effort on one's behalf to dissolve any relationship with peace will benefit both participants in their overall well-being and reduce the residual effects of the unrest in the relationship.

Casual relationships with co-workers, neighbours, or perhaps an acquaintance or a close friend we may see on a regular basis can deliver many challenges for us as well. We may have people we see out of necessity, but many times, the relationships evolve to a point where we may enjoy spending time together. If it remains solely a relationship out of necessity, often we may not apply the effort to get along as much as with closer relationships. Unfortunately, the result of our behaviours or words can lead to unsettling feelings and ultimately can create an environment that is not inviting at all, though it is an environment that we must return to on a recurring basis. That's not a good place to be; even if we simply ignore the individual, there is a definite effect upon our spirit, whether we want to admit it or not.

Ultimately, any type of relationship has an unquestionable

effect upon each and every one of us, and each of us decides which relationships we commit to and which ones we abandon. Yes, we can in fact chose to not speak or interact with close family members, other family relations, co-workers, or neighbours, but our interactions and working through differences is what makes the world go around. When we dissolve relationships not conducive to peace or hold them in turmoil, we create unrest in ourselves and the others involved. Spiritually, it is in our best interest to embrace and accept the challenges we face in our multitude of relationships or remove ourselves from relationships in a fashion conducive to peace.

Our continual experiences and our multitude of relationships make up a major portion of all of our days, of all of our lives. Many bring us great pleasure and a great deal of satisfaction and give us sense of purpose and happiness, and we're glad to be alive. On the other side of the coin, we have experiences and relations that are not welcoming, but when we can embrace them as they are and know that ultimately growth is the result, we can feel ourselves in a good spot upon the eternal ladder. We can know that we are indeed an active and intricate participant in the most fascinating race—the human race!

Chapter 3

THE MOST FASCINATING RACE

The Most Fascinating Race

At the front gate, upon the white line

The race is now ready to start.

Fortitude of each, that eagerly wait,

To give all, with all of their heart.

Tension hangs thick, amid the dense air

Outcome being far, far from known.

The only thing certain, at finish of race-

Is one victor, and one victor alone.

The race is then launched, and pressure does mount,

The battle then goes tooth and nail.

Through every mind, throughout entire race

To come second, is surely to fail.

The contest builds up, and ending is near,
Each entry strives more to prevail.
The finish line, now clear to the sight,
Its sole purpose, is but to assail.

Finish line crossed and victor declared,
The crowd pleased with effort of all.
Winner steps up, the others aside
With heads down, amid their shortfall.

A Voice in the crowd then inquires aloud,
Can you give Me a moment to speak?
I've something to say, a message of Love-
For all, those strong, and those weak.

The Voice carried on, in celestial guise
And the crowd stood in silence and awe.
No one could believe of what their ears heard,
Or that, of what their eyes saw.

Sound and vision coalesce to Light
As the message continued to flow.
There is but one race in which everyone wins,
It is this, I would like you to know.

No second or third, all participants win,

This, understood through My grace.

This fascinating journey, of which all do win,

Is that known, known as "Human Race."

A large portion of the truth we learn in our youth and continue to experience throughout our lives is that we must strive to conquer, strive to do our utmost best, strive to win. It is typically ingrained in us from an early age and an inherent characteristic born into many. From a very young age, we want to win attention from parents, family, and other toddlers. As we progress in youth, we are encouraged or we want to win in games and sports, various competitions, school grades, and other activities we experience alone and with others. In our teens, we look to excel in any activities or events that can elevate our popularity, many times activities deemed or perceived as good or bad. As we enter adulthood, we attempt or strive for all of the perceived truths shared with us, which we reviewed in an earlier chapter—the truths and the wins revealed and shared by those who came before us, including parents, family, teachers, and other figures of influence or authority in our impressionable years.

Realistically, there are physical, intellectual, and emotional roadblocks for all of us in one way or another; no one can do all things and be all things in the flesh. In many cases, those shaping and moulding us recognize our limitations and encouragement to work with what we have prevails. But in many other situations, our limitations may not be recognized or may be ignored, and the push is on to excel in a certain sport, a certain career path, a certain goal that will eventually place a child firmly in the winner's circle. The degree of shaping, moulding, coaching, and encouraging is ultimately affected by the awareness of those surrounding us in our youth, and all guidance is given to the utmost best of one's ability in any given time and space. We all do the best we can with the awareness we possess on any rung of the ladder we happen to be on—parents, family, and all other influences included. Our predecessors prominently want only the best for us and give us the guidance, direction, and support that they have within them, based on their current awareness.

How often do we see children encouraged, influenced, and pushed in a direction to become a professional athlete or a doctor or lawyer, often with the youth believing themselves that this is the direction they want to go in. The intention is noble, and in many situations, the goal can come to fruition, but often when the mark is missed, it stirs and perpetuates confusion, frustration, disappointment, and many other forms of negative feelings for both the parent and the offspring. The motives are honourable, as perception dictates that by hitting the mark, we win, both the encouraging parent or other and the child.

There are many environments conducive to letting the chips fall where they may, so to speak, and parents and other influential people support youth decisions with varying degrees of liberation. With increased awareness, liberation and freedom prevail, and walking upon the passage of existence can lend itself to victories, sometimes real and many times perceived. To elaborate, if our targets are hit, we may still not feel that we have won; we may still have a sense within that happiness and contentment are eluding us to varying degrees. To have a sense of true victory, all the other components of knowing our true selves must be in place to a certain degree.

Throughout our lives, we are bombarded with the perceived ideas, concepts, and images of winning and what victory looks, smells, feels, sounds, and tastes like. The collective ego, society, exudes the belief that we win with what we drive, the house we live in, the position we hold, and the perfume or cologne or clothes we wear. We are many times led to believe that status and possessions are the path to happiness, to any degree. To some, the realization of owning a home, the ability to comfortably provide for our families, and the ability to maintain continual employment create a winning attitude, a winning feeling. Others only realize success or victory when they obtain stardom, extreme financial success, or other types of extreme recognition in one way or another. But regardless of what goals people set and obtain, in many cases, they measure victory by setting themselves, as the victor, apart from others, setting themselves apart from the crowd. Victory is recognized by being, having, or knowing more than another, and we have won the game of life in our own eyes.

This can lead to an overall sense of well-being many times in our lives and in many situations. But these feelings ultimately rest upon the brow of the ego, and we experience other times and other human beings who inevitably make us feel we do not measure up. We once again feel or experience that maybe, just maybe, we haven't won after all. This can ultimately drive us to pursue additional goals, additional targets toward victory, toward putting us back on the top of the heap once again. Many chase this illusion until the latest possible stages in life. It can also discourage us and hold us in an emotional pattern of unrest, telling us we can never win and we will never be what others are, and what we think we should be. Realistically, many of us become trapped in this pattern for most or all of our lives. Various levels of defeat are instilled within us, and existence, not vigorous living, becomes the stage we set our feet upon day in and day out.

As this realistic phenomenon has occurred and continues to occur in our human existence, we typically experience it without us really even knowing. Yes, people often claim that they are happy with what they have, that they know what brings happiness, that they know the real components of victory. But for the most part, it can and does exist upon the plane of our subconscious, and at this level, it can be extremely impenetrable and unchangeable. At this level, we are unknowingly held in a pattern of comparison and fear. Our ability to break the cycle arises only through the combination of our own experiences and awareness experienced through Divine grace. Ultimately victory is experienced intermittently, never continually.

Often, we establish our sense of self, our sense of victory, and our sense of winning in our daily communication. We persist in our verbal interactions to win an argument or to force our mental position or opinions upon others. Again, most times, we do so subconsciously, unaware that we have our feet firmly planted in our own soil of truth. We at times become so intimately and intensely involved in verbal discrepancies that we find ourselves speaking words that may not in fact hold truth, in the name of firmly establishing our position. Through experiences such as these, we sometimes find ourselves after the interaction, aware of an inconsistency in the facts, in our words, but pride and the overall sense of the importance of winning prevails. We can become so stubborn at times that winning at any cost becomes our reality, and we further cloud our truth of real understanding.

Illusive victory takes so many forms, often people in the same circle of life will subconsciously target that which they know will put them on top in one way or another. Perhaps people will use humour at every available moment to establish their own little personal victories. They become known among their peers as the jokester and can always be counted on for a laugh. With this embedded in their being, after a period of time, it becomes who they are to varying degrees. Tremendous pain and unrest can lie just below their surface, but every new little victory pulls the wool of self-deception over their eyes once again, as the source of the pain is never really addressed.

Others develop a sense of victory, a sense of winning when they are the outspoken one, the smart one, the sexy one, or any other one in the circle. They seek the sense of victory on a regular basis through subconscious comparison. We often take actions and speak words to initiate others to remind us of our special talents, abilities, possessions, or appearances in order to ring the bell of illusive victory one more time!

And although we can come to count on these little victories on a regular basis, they may really only hold our head above water, as we see and are reminded of all the personal victories of the others within our circle. We are one as an individual, and our circle at work, in our community, and in our family consists of many, many others. And ultimately for every one of our little victories, we see victories tenfold in the accumulations of all others. We hear the bell of victory for ourselves perhaps a few times a day and hear it hundreds of times a day for those around us. We continually move from winner to loser, up, down, and all around, never feeling real peace at our centre, never knowing firmly within ourselves that we are okay exactly as we are-sometimes consciously, but most times subconsciously.

For those with the continual drive to win, the chase is on to find new talents, new challenges, and new opportunities to ring our bell more frequently—the new job, the new sport, the new car, the new spouse. Unknowingly, we search every nook and cranny, we leave no stone unturned, in our quest for victory. In many cases, and if motives and actions are aligned with Love, we can find success, fulfilment, and joy in new challenges, opportunities, or life situations. But all too often, we experience cycles of confusion and discontent, as the bell simply cannot ring at the frequency required or desired. We continue to chase our illusory heaven but many times remain in our illusory hell.

For the more passive type, the drive to win simply dissolves or dries up and unfulfilled acceptance and existence evolve as the way of their world. They trod through life with a sombre demeanour, and the thought of falling asleep each night brings a sense of relief and waking each day a sense of fear. Life eventually provides no real highs or lows but simply a constant state of unwavering disappointment. Hope has fallen by the wayside, and we teeter on a most undesirable rung upon the ladder.

Whether we actively seek to find new victories or raise the white flag at the game of life, our overall sense of hope can diminish and patterns of escape can develop. These patterns can bring instant gratification for short periods of time- and can and do ultimately drive us deeper into the pit of despair. Substance abuse, gambling, notches in our sexual belts, or perhaps our eating habits—when victory eludes us to a certain degree of despair, the quick fix will do the trick for us on the drop of a dime. We can push the thoughts of defeat deep within ourselves, with a sense of satisfaction, relief, and pleasure. We can take a vacation from our thoughts, a vacation from our perceived problems, and lie on the beach of ecstasy for but a short time. When we visit and revisit our vacation destination on a regular basis, our once loved destination can throw us into the depths of pain even further, into patterns of overindulgence and addiction.

Every thought, every feeling, every experience we partake in not knowing who we really are eventually and continually brings us to the point of comparison, the point of striving for victory, or the point of throwing in the towel. None of us walking the face of the earth escapes this dilemma, whether we think we do or not. It is only through knowledge of our true Self that the routine of comparison and the illusive victory sought through our unseeing eyes can begin to change and we can begin to have a new awareness, a new place on life's eternal ladder.

And just how do we go about obtaining a sense of our true Self? There are a multitude of paths, but ultimately all paths strip us of our illusions of how the world really works and the illusion of separation. Every experience we encounter is taking us in the direction of this awareness, and it is simultaneously occurring for each and every one of us. We cannot escape this existence, as we learn lessons with either an effort to attain awareness or persistent denial and continued effort to hide our inner truth. One way or another, we all get there!

When we do arrive, wins and losses simply become experiences to learn from, grow from, and reflect upon at a future point in time, to remind us of the person we want to be and the one we do not want to be. We recognize our real victories, our true victories, when we can touch the spirit of others and remind them in some way of who they really are. We can rub elbows with individuals of high status or those living in the streets, and with the sinners or the saints.

The importance of the victories we once sought tends to go by the wayside. We begin to know the ultimate victory, which we work to attain and lovingly and willingly migrate toward. We begin to sense internally that it has been our target from day one. This target evades all of us to one degree or another throughout our time in the flesh. We begin to dismiss the notion that to always come first, to always be the best, to always be on top in one way or another is how we win in the game of life. We begin to accept and comprehend that there really is no difference in winning or losing, that they are both only experiences guiding us in the direction of self-knowledge and thus knowledge of all others. Right or wrong, good or bad, win or lose—all begin to dissipate upon the rungs of awareness.

We still flow in the direction of our goals in which we want to succeed, whether it be excelling in a career path, becoming the champion at our tennis club, or perhaps being named employee of the month. We do not give up at the game of life; we simply surrender to the feelings of victory or defeat in anything we attempt or do, and to our past illusion that when someone wins, someone else loses. When we do experience victory of any sort, we do so with a new sense of appreciation, a new sense of gratitude, one that puts the credit in a much larger Entity than ourselves.

Very often, the successes we once put so much weight upon actually become easier to attain and much more enjoyable with our new sense of true victory. Again, there is nothing wrong with wanting our personal best, and whether our goals come to fruition or not, we can know a sense of peace and higher purpose. We can know that, win or lose, we are loved beyond our wildest dreams. We can know the universe is rooting for all of us to ultimately win, and win we shall!

Chapter 4

THE PROVERBIAL STRAW

The Proverbial Straw

Born unto turmoil, the struggles of youth
Answers, unknown to most all.
Trials, tribulations, in search of the truth,
Eternal past, we cannot recall.

The play of life unfolds, one scene at a time
The stage continually set through the years.
The ladder of enchantment, our intended climb-
We but fall, in affliction and in tears.

A desolate battle, fought hard in each mortal,
Reliance on self to prevail.
Looking unto mind, avoiding the portal-
Which looks in, upon precious grail.

A multitude of quandaries, do come one by one,
Self-made answers, none left to withdraw.
Sanctified healing through Grace has begun,
When placed, the proverbial straw.

The proverbial straw that broke camel's back
A blessing beyond wildest dreams.
Gazing within, no absence or lack
Looking out, is nothing as it seems.

Eternal strength, now coursing the veins,
Of Being, of life, and of Truth.
Driving forward, with new set of reins
Propelled forth, toward Infinite youth.

The straw that broke the camel's back is the situation, incident, or experience that finds us in a position that we can no longer tolerate or do not want to accept. It puts us at a crossroads or a breaking point and indicates a necessary change. Typically, when one hears, "That's the last straw," one knows or feels that one has been pushed to the limit, the gig is up, and they have acted, spoken, or behaved in a manner that now beckons the arrival of an undesirable action or an undesirable consequence. But upon the eternal ladder, the last straw does not bring about an undesirable action, outcome, or consequence. The last straw can bring us to a point of new awareness, a point that catapults us to a different rung of understanding and is experienced as a blessing in disguise. Upon the ladder, the multitude of experiences serves to strip away illusion and ultimately bring us face to face with truth. The cumulative effects of these experiences form, gather, build, and ultimately burst in our subconscious, bringing to the light of consciousness a new field of vision, a new awareness of ourselves, our brothers and sisters, and the world we live in.

We ultimately arrive at this stage of our spiritual growth and understanding with our behaviours, actions, beliefs, and experiences, and this point of awareness varies from person to person, soul to soul. Some are born into this world in which little experience is required to hit the breaking point, and in reality as we know it, many never reach it in their current life or existence. An existence does ultimately occur for all of us in Eternity in which a new understanding invades our being and we truly do see the world through a different set of eyes and know Love at our core. In other experiences, the dawn of awakening comes to full light through other means—continuous and wholehearted practice of religion, meditation, or goodwill, to name a few. Of these, I cannot speak, as it has been the accumulation of experiences, perceived as both good and bad, that has lifted the curtain of truth on my own stage of awareness. Ultimately, whatever leads us to awaken, it is experience in one way, shape, or form. This is why we are here; this is why we exist with our feet upon the ground of life as we know it.

The straws that accumulate within, the memories and experiences that shape our present and future awareness, can and do frequently consist of a wide array of subject matter, such as people in our circle of life, employment experiences, or the environment in which we live. The subject matter evolves around all of our interactions and our relationships with others and ourselves. Realistically, it is any subject matter we experience in each of our daily lives and not a singular matter but many. We can and do see a multitude of paths to self-awareness, and typically the paths contain bits and pieces of all the realms or our experiences, our existence.

This is not to say that it is only our hardships or challenges that accumulate to bring us to the point of psychic change. It is the accumulation of *all* our experiences that awakens us. Good times, good memories, and good experiences are certainly a large part of our healing, as it is the experiences that we encounter and that touch our hearts that give us the hope, the drive, and the reference points to where we want to be on a consistent basis. We can experience great joy when we or others in our circle have a child, a family party, a barbecue, or any other event that brings a smile to our face and love into our hearts. Or we can experience pleasure in a bike ride, going to a movie, going out for dinner, or any other experience that gives us a sense of happiness and contentment for the duration of the event and experience. We experience what we enjoy in our lives, what brings us a sense of well-being, and in a sense, this is what brings the pain and hurt to light in the times of challenge, the times we wish we did not have to experience. We now perceive both pleasant and unpleasant experiences.

We ultimately chase the pleasure and the joy in our lives, in hopes of evading the pain and the hardships we all inevitably encounter through experiences that ultimately cause us to question the worthiness, integrity, and good within ourselves and the people around us close, distant, and unknown. Experiences that occur from very early on in our lives in early childhood and become the pinnacle point in our existence from which we begin to lose our innocence and cast judgment upon ourselves and those around us, based on what we encounter; and those that lead us to our destructive sense of separation.

I can vividly remember times in my youth when I felt so alive, so free, so inspired—running through fields in the spring, playing with friends in the neighbourhood, listening to the water flow under the tracks at the three tunnels, and throwing a baseball in the yard with my father. The point comes for all of us when this freedom is lost, our sense of separation develops, and we begin to learn the ways of the world through the experience and direction of those who came before us—our parents, teachers, and the like. As outlined in an earlier chapter, this is when our perception of all that is right or wrong and good or bad enters our consciousness. This is our entry into the proverbial garden of good and evil!

At this point, we evolve to label our experiences as pleasurable or not, good or bad, right or wrong. It is at this point that we begin to reference our perceived good or bad experiences, and life takes us down the many paths that unfold in front of us. We chase our dreams, our goals, our perceived happiness and truth, and typically rely on answers from ourselves or those around us when difficult or problematic times unfold. Many times, we simply push down the emotions, swallow the pain, and flash an erroneous smile, as we have been told to get up and dust ourselves off all too often. We have been told to suck it up, be a man, don't be a baby, and brush it off. All too often, we turn inward and search out our own answers or look to evade the experience, evade the pain, and trudge on. We enter the plane of simple existence and tread forward with decreasing hope of ever getting off. The real joy of life often evades us, or many times disappears altogether.

We can be trapped in this existence sometimes indefinitely, or we can flow into and out of this melancholy condition many times throughout our lives. Inevitably, we can go up or down in our overall sense of well-being, and we continually ride the roller coaster of life. We may seek escape through addiction, sexual escapades, thrill-seeking, material gain, or status - or simply withdrawal from our circle or family. We carry on to varying degrees of contentment, varying degrees of satisfaction, but a true sense of joy, a true sense of awareness, a true sense of love often evades us.

Ultimately, it is our relationships and our interactions and experiences within each of our relationships that test the waters of awareness and accumulate the straws of discontentment. Each of us has varying degrees of communication or interaction with others. Some have a multitude of relationships or contacts with others, some have very few, and some have none, other than a visit to a doctor, a telephone call from a solicitor, or perhaps short dialogue at a supermarket with the cashier. Our personal interactions with others-and therefore ourselves, are the primary source of the accumulation of pain within, and whether it be an intimate or casual relationship, these daily interactions find their spot in the depths of our subconscious and build upon our stack of straws.

Running from our painful interactions and relationships is a choice often taken and seen as the path to rectify the hurt. In many cases, this may hold some truth, such as in relationships that contain physical violence, but ultimately, remaining in, enduring, or leaving any type of relationship serves only one purpose, which is that of our own growth. Every relationship and every interaction within the relationship move us toward Light and Love, or darkness and fear. When we run from any relationship and are not looking at our part in the breakdown, we drive ourselves into further darkness.

In chapter 2, we touched briefly on the common result of unhappiness in many intimate relationships. The result discussed was that of separation, of finding a new relationship to end the pain of the one now in existence and to end our suffering, which we can or chose not to tolerate any longer. Do relationships exist in which this result is of necessity? Absolutely. Do relationships exist that are abandoned and thrown by the wayside because one or both participants can't accept the idiosyncrasies of the other? Most certainly.

It is the words, actions, and overall demeanours of those who surround us the most that stir the changes required within ourselves. Our toughest relationships are those that cast the light of truth upon the shadows deep within ourselves. When we do not reflect within and find the place that can move us toward resolve and understanding, the straws compound- and ripple out into every other relation and interaction within our lives. Typically, we hold on to and revisit the pain once endured in our relationships and internally justify the endings we created. We ultimately build upon the actions and words undertaken by others and tear down or forget our own. We ultimately reinforce our position of being right and the other's position of being wrong, resulting in both of us experiencing yet another perceived example or experience of separation.

These types of relationships can indeed be very difficult to endure, but they can also position us upon a different rung of understanding when we work through them and come out the other end of the many trying moments. The results of any challenging interaction, any trying time, or any mental or emotional hurdle we face head-on and work through add straws of strength to our repertoire and move us toward a better understanding of life and ultimately of Love. In times when these challenges are faced head-on and worked through, but whereby true resolve and forgiveness have not occurred, migration will lean toward further separation, further darkness, and further fear.

So how is it that our personal relationships and the experiences within them happen to have the most impact, the most significance to our understanding and awareness of our lives, ourselves, and all others? Every unresolved, misunderstood, or misperceived experience we partake in continually compounds our sense of separation and darkness and our tendency toward further words and actions that lead to yet more pain, hurt, and anger. We can literally spin on the perpetual wheel of illusion, accumulating straw after straw of discontent. We can meander through all the days of our lives, or with any luck, with any grace, the proverbial straw gets lovingly placed upon us. This is the final straw, the final curtain, the final obstacle that opens our eyes wide open to the truth!

Our life experiences and personal interactions can hold us to varying degrees of contentment, varying degrees of fulfilment, or varying degrees of simple existence, whereas life proceeds with us in an overall state of discontent and malaise. Many view hard times or unhappiness as a curse, but when we can no longer find any answers within ourselves or from others in our circle or professional sources, we have but one direction to go to really break through the shell of existence and discover the truth. It is the point in our life experience that the straw can in fact break the camel's back, where we again look into ourselves, not into our minds, but into our hearts; where we again look outside ourselves, not to those in our circle or outsiders, but to the realm of infinity, in which everything yet nothing is contained. This is where we find Truth, Love, and ultimately, our true Selves.

It is here that we can begin to discover, experience, and know at our core the Source of every answer to every question that has occupied the hearts and minds of every human being from the beginning of time as we know it. Another fantastic band with a deep understanding of this is the Steve Miller Band. In the song "Jungle Love," a line in one verse tells us

"the question to everyone's answer, is usually asked from within" [6]

We all have a longing, a deep desire, and a deep question within us. Who are we, where did we come from, and why are we here? If these questions have not come to the forefront of consciousness within you, rest assured, they will. They are within us all, to varying degrees of subtlety. Eternity brings us all down our own path to truth, and we all experience our own proverbial straw.

When the proverbial straw finally breaks the camel's back, we begin to see the world in a different light. We develop a radical shift in our understanding of ourselves and our world. The curtain of separation is lovingly lifted, and we return to the sense of joy and innocence we once experienced as a child, the sense of wonder and awe, the sense of life coursing through our bodies long since forgotten. We can now comprehend and understand the totality of our universe

---

[6] Written by Morris Day, Prince Rogers Nelson • Copyright © Universal Music Publishing Group

and everything contained within it- and recognize ourselves in everything and everyone we experience.

Our accumulated pain, anger, and discontent melt from us with a new awareness of Love. Love that has been with us and part of us from the beginning. The emotional hangovers that may have existed for immensely long periods of time will dissipate as the voice of the universe gently and lovingly whispers that it is now time to awaken. We can now reflect on our entire unconscious life and know that every incident, every interaction, every experience was necessary to land us in this present moment. We can now experience life through our Being, not through the lenses of perception, interpreted and manipulated by the incessant ego. We will know our perfection and that of all of our brothers and sisters as well.

Our new perspective calls us back to our true nature, the nature we have lost in the innocence of youth, the nature that was driven deep within when we experienced and learned the ways of our world. This is the point where unlearning occurs, and we could never be more ecstatic with the realization that we truly know nothing! With a new awareness, a new understanding of ourselves and our world, we now rely on the unseen force that embraces and guides everything to reteach us through Love with every new experience we encounter each moment.

Do all of our challenges, all of our questions, all of our uncertainties disappear? Absolutely not! Do we now have a different perspective and understanding when any new experience or interaction challenges our peace of mind? Absolutely! We can now know at our core that at any time peace is not present within us, we are entering an experience or interaction in which fear is playing upon our heartstrings and we are forgetting the Love within us that never really leaves. As discussed in an earlier chapter, in fight-or-flight situations, it is very difficult, if not impossible, to find our centre. Total peace may not be an option, but upon reflection, we know growth is inevitable no matter what may cross our path.

With our new shift in awareness, with our new position on the ladder of life, our experiences shift from "Why is this happening to me?" to "This is happening as required, for the growth of all involved." We are all in this together, always have been, and always will be, and with this realization, we know that endeavouring to bring love, compassion, and understanding into every experience and interaction is at the forefront of intention. We now look into the mirror of life and see ourselves everywhere, in everything!

Chapter 5

THE MIRROR

The Mirror

A family heirloom, a coveted treasure
Passed lovingly from experience to youth.
Beyond all illusion, one day to discover
It's reflection, to reveal only the Truth.

The precious mirror, so loved by young child,
A possession held high in regard.
Its soothing presence, emitting peace, composure
Emotional haven, a comforting safeguard.

An impression of beauty, cast back to bright windows,
Through which life was looked out upon each day.
The fairest of features, the innocence of youth,
In young mind, to eternally stay.

Time shifts but forward, alluring image subsides,
The reflection then beckoned no more.
Mirror bitterly abandoned, sentient pain,
No appearance now left to adore.

Anger and anguish consume every cell,
Dissolution, afraid and alone.
The misdeeds of others, the hurt, the pain
Her mind, her presence, can't atone.

Hope long diminished in compassion or love,
Hardened eyes, once bright now stone grey.
Sense of life, of purpose, of joy
A wrong turn, gone vastly astray.

A vision invades slumber, from relations long past,
To speak of the mirror now forsaken.
"Take one more real look, a favour to us—
Tomorrow, the day you Awaken.

Morning arose, the woman sought the mirror
The reflection, now radiant with Love.
No solitary image, but fusion of all
Now seen, with help from above.

The mirror again cherished, the vision now real

Its worth, far greater than before.

An image of Oneness, the mirror's true reflection,

The portal, to Life's heavenly door.

In earlier chapters, we touched on the loss of our innocence in our youth, the loss of the wonder and amazement of our world, as we move forward in our early years. We move through infancy to toddlerhood into youth, and at some point in our evolution, we fall asleep from our natural state and remain so to varying degrees throughout our lives. We learn the ways of the world from those guiding and influencing our lives, and also from within, and find ourselves in a state of separation, individuality, and difference from those around us. We typically learn that when we behave, speak, or act in varying manners, we are being "bad" or committing "sin." We are letting down our parents, ourselves, and ultimately God.

We develop a sense of guilt, and we hide, conceal, or deny our perceived misdoings to avoid the feelings generated by the words we hear from others as a result of our behaviour. We experience feelings of unworthiness, as words of fear, lack, and hurt are directed toward us. Words and actions that generate verbal, physical, and emotional punishment and omit any true sense of Love. They land upon us as the recipient in our youth, and are generated to help change the inappropriate behaviours and actions of others- when we ourselves become the point of delivery in our later years of life as parents or other influential roles we may participate in.

We lose our sense of Self, that which we come into the world with, our natural state. The degree of loss of this sense, of our awareness, is ultimately affected by our eternal past and our understanding of unconditional Love emanating our world, our universe, and the entire cosmos. Some may relate this to reincarnation or karma. Simply put,

I relate it to our past upon the realm of what we look upon as time. Ultimately, our awareness perpetually grows within our spirit, and our spirit is as eternal as God and the universe itself. When we feel this, when we know this within, time as we know it ceases to exist, except clock time, which exists out of necessity in our daily lives.

As we come out of our natural state, and life evolves for all of us as it does, our loss of our innocence, our loss of our true nature imminently occurs, in accordance with the Divine plan we are all a pertinent part of. If we are born once again into this material world, there is no escape; there is no denying this fate in which we are cast upon the seas of separation and oceans of despair to one degree or another.

In the material world as we know it, as we lose our innocence, appearance is everything to many. Appearance, physically, emotionally, and materially, comes to the forefront of our attention on a regular basis. Our egos hold us hostage in an incessant state of comparison, whether we want to admit it or not, as we see the world through the eyes of separation. For the most part, the occurrence is within our subconscious, below the radar if you will. For the most part, our incessant judgments occur without us even knowing.

In all of our lives, we recurrently reflect upon our image, our point of reference, from both a physical and emotional perspective, in the mirror of separation. In a physical sense, we typically delve into our reflection as we awaken each day to brush our teeth, comb our hair, or wash our face. We face the man or woman in the mirror to tidy up and face the world for yet another day. Spot checks throughout our day are commonplace, as we look for assurance our hair is in place and our shirts are tucked in. We cast our eyes upon the mirror with full admiration or repulsion and everything else in between. We like what we see, or we dislike what we see, but it is most often our feelings, our emotions that gauge the range of this experience.

More so than the physical reflection we seek out each day, perhaps tenfold, twentyfold, a hundredfold, it is our emotional reflections that occur sometimes consciously- but mostly subconsciously. We unceasingly, subconsciously look at ourselves and others, our situations, and the situations of others, and the reflections filter back to impact our perception of ourselves, our egos. We can at times feel as small as an ant or as large as an elephant and everything in between. We look into the mirror of life, and our eyes and emotions bestow a dull or brilliant reflection, depending on our state of well-being.

As we continually bombard our inner selves with variable feelings of self-worth from one day to the next, we become internally overwhelmed, and this ultimately leads us down paths that become definitive moments on our current rung. Cumulative feelings of unworthiness, despair, hurt, or anger can drive us into a state of depression. Cumulative feelings of victory, arrogance, and being better than others can drive us hard into the wall of pride, whereby recuperation can often be long but is always necessary.

"When self-importance is driving, a devastating collision is imminent"

Throughout our experiences and throughout our lives, we travel many roads that have us in variable states of well-being, and many among us can hold the line, stay in the middle of the road, and avoid the extreme peaks or valleys to a certain degree. There is no escaping the peaks and valleys altogether, as we all face times within our lives when we feel a degree of diminished self-worth and a degree of feeling like we just don't quite measure up, consciously and subconsciously.

In chapter 1, we touched on the cumulative effects of our individual ego, as dictated by each and every interaction and situation we experience. We can fluctuate between feelings of importance and feelings of unworthiness, no doubt. Inevitably though, we reflect upon ourselves, our world, and those around us through the mirror of separation, the mirror of individuality, and ultimately the mirror of misperception. There is really no escaping the reflections we see and feel until we ultimately cease to identify with our mind, our ego, and what it is telling us.

Telling us we have been lied to and cheated, we are not what we should be and what we ought to be, and what we are not. Daily interactions, situations, and experiences occur, and our self-worth, our self-esteem and overall well-being can fluctuate and change like the weather. Our emotional state and acceptance of ourselves, our surroundings, and our lives in general hinge on our subconscious reflection in the mirror of comparison and judgment. We compare appearances, statuses, and material possessions. We judge others' actions, words, and performance.

We go to trial day in and day out, and when the jury returns into the courtroom of our minds, our egos, we are convicted to a state of worthiness when we win and unworthiness when we lose. Yes, we can see many whom we perceive as continually winning in the game of life, but if they remain attached to mind identification, the subconscious ego, victory never truly arrives. There is always one more trial, one more required win around the corner, one more trophy, one more acquisition, one more victory to attain. Even the most successful individuals fail to evade comparison, as we all eventually interact with others our ego perceives as better than, smarter than, or more than in any other characteristic or quality in which we feel lack. There is no escaping this, at least subconsciously, and refutation points straight in the direction of denial. Anyone who looks within will feel an inkling of truth in this, if he or she can look deep enough.

Also, the perceived victories with individuals such as these come with losses in other areas of life that are often ignored or downplayed. We continually strive to get ahead financially in our occupation or business and have to make sacrifices—no ifs, ands, or buts. We claim our efforts are undertaken to take care of our families and their well-being, whereby we often see the breakdown of the family unit as a result of time away and overall commitment to the family unit. Balance is not maintained, and the unit can dissolve literally with divorce or separation or exist in a state of discontent or lack in one form or another. Without balance and with all involved tied to egoic identification, suffering ultimately occurs. Spouses and children develop feelings of lack—lack of love, lack of worthiness, lack of well-being. The perceived victory with one member of the unit ultimately produces effects that can ripple to great lengths in the pond of life of others.

As in business or financial pursuits, this breakdown can occur in many other situations. Individuals can devote themselves to, commit to, and win at a sport, a hobby, or any other undertaking. Winning inevitably comes at a price, and many pay the price without the blink of an eye. The perceived victories outweigh relational losses, and life goes on, pegging us on top and placing others' feelings and sense of well-being at the bottom. Our goals, our victories come first; without them, our sense of worth cannot be and continue to be established. We pursue our goals often into the realm of loss, loss that we often continually deny.

There are others who experience the feeling of unworthiness, of not quite stacking up; they feel that life has challenged them and they have failed. This overall feeling of lack of well-being can start early in life or set in at any stage, depending on our journey upon the ladder. The jury returns day in and day out, and the verdicts continually stack against us, one after the other—guilty, guilty, guilty! You lose, lose, lose! When the cumulative effect of our perceived losses outweighs our victories or we experience more perceived losses than victories, our overall sense of well-being positions us upon the plane of simple existence, an existence noted in earlier chapters that lacks any real excitement, enthusiasm, or inspiration.

We reflect often in our own mirror of illusion, our own self. But we also subconsciously, incessantly peer into the lives of others around us, determining our self-worth or lack thereof – and the worth, value, and judgment of anything else we bring into our thoughts of those upon whom we cast our eyes and our minds. We often feel jilted, taken for a ride, and done wrong by. As discussed earlier, we often dissolve interactions or relationships with individuals who upset our apple cart after deeming the pain or effort to repair the relationship is too great, often without forgiveness.

When we do not forgive, we hold the alleged perpetrators in the black book of our mind. They have lied to us, they have stolen from us, they have violated our space or our being, and they are then held in low regard in our perception of human decency. Many in life are scarred time after time with this affliction, as hearts harden, skin thickens, and feelings of compassion and understanding diminish with each new similar experience. We become cold, cynical, and often very unpleasant, as faith in our brothers and sisters recurrently depletes.

The misdoings of others, whether actual or not, further contributes to our own internal dull reflection, as when we look at others, we are really only looking at ourselves! When our thoughts reduce the value or importance of any human being or we cast judgment upon people based on their words, actions, or appearance, we are throwing the boomerang of illusion, the boomerang of pain, one more time, and it inevitably returns to us and embeds within our own core.

Whether it be the reflection of ourselves or our vision of others, we can develop a deep sense of anguish within, which can ripple into the lives of others as well, as our feelings of lack, defeat, and unworthiness create the aura that surrounds us and penetrates those of others. We emanate this sense toward and into others, and our state can then affect or become that of those around us. Our spouses, siblings, parents, children, friends, or anyone else within our circle can be affected to varying degrees. When the pain of our affliction is recognized in others, we often isolate ourselves and retreat in knowing the hurt we are causing. With good intentions in our hearts, we cast ourselves and those around us into further inner turmoil, as any unresolved, continual lack of well-being festers and grows within all involved. The unwanted, unappealing reflection in our own mirror ultimately creeps into the reflection of others, and adds to their own subconscious anguish.

Upon our current rung, we establish perceived victory or defeat but often variable states between the two. Whether our overall experience is greater victory than defeat or vice versa, the reflection we return to within our minds inevitably and continually contributes to our sense of self. With our perceived sense of self, there is an effect on those around us, when all involved are held captive by their minds and their egos. With our perceived separation, someone always has to lose when someone wins, and losses in one individual often contribute to the losses of others close within our circle of life. The mirror of separation, the mirror of perception, holds us in a state of illusion, in which no one truly wins peace within.

Victory can only be claimed and felt at the core of being, when the reflection we experience is illuminated with Love and with unity. When we are held hostage by our minds, by our egos, the reflections seen within and without emanate our individuality, our separation, and ultimately our illusion. This reflection always brings pain, discontentment, and inner anguish with no means of escape, whether one believes so or not. Some may convince themselves and perhaps feel that pain, discontentment, and inner anguish do not exist within them. This only contributes further to the illusion of the mind, as at this point, emotions have been pushed into the bowels of our existence.

The opportunity, the good fortune beyond our wildest dreams, to experience the reflection cast from the mirror of Love, appears only when we discover the truth, discover our true Self. And as outlined earlier, it is only through stripping the layers of illusion from ourselves, moving away from all that is not real, and unlearning much of what was passed down to us from those before us that we can come to this realization.

The reflection radiating into, throughout, and all around us now contains unity of all we see, and we now feel a part of all at our core, not separate and alone, as when we are held captive by the ego. This moment in time does come for us all and is the divine purpose for our walk upon the path of life, the path that leads to time and one's Self.

Chapter 6

OF TIME AND ONE'S SELF

Of Time and One's Self

A day, month, or year, the time upon earth
A measure by our human race.
Infinite death and infinite birth
Lay outside perceived time, perceived space.

Infinite thoughts ring loud upon my Self
They call to look deep, deep within.
All of my feelings, my knowledge, my wealth-
Results of the Being I have been.

The clock in my mind, ticks time to go home,
To a place in the realm of the heart.
Upon the earth body I journey and roam,
Assured I'll return to my start.

All that I am, and all that I'll be
Revealed but one thought at a time.
The ultimate quest, of being form-free,
Doth result in the state of sublime.

To know one's Self, be it known or not
Is our destiny, in form upon earth.
Arrival in whole, of this conscious thought
Does reveal one's phenomenal worth!

At an early age, we learn about clock time—the seconds, minutes, hours, days, and years. We learn the importance of time, and it becomes a fundamental aspect of our existence early on in life. It is one of the basic teachings in the early school years—at least it was in my experience. I can still remember pouring over all the sheets of paper with the empty clock faces, with continual effort to draw the hands onto the clock that matched the directive of the teacher. It's right up there with the ABCs and 123's, no doubt! We learn to pay extreme attention to it, as we need to be to school on time, to work on time, to here, there, and everywhere on time. We evolve and learn to save time, waste time, and check time on a continual basis, being ever concerned that we are going to be on time. In accordance with our everyday commitments, appointments, and the like, time has purpose, and adherence to our schedules is of course important. We know the repercussions of missing appointments or events or being late for work. We hurt ourselves, our loved ones, our employers, and others when we cannot meet clock time commitments, and in this light, honouring time is essential.

We are also indoctrinated in our early years to cherish and honour time in a different manner, as it is limited for us in our lives upon the earth. We are yet again led by those who come before us to have a game plan, so that we make the most of the time we have in the so-called critical periods of our existence. We are directed to meet someone to marry and have children with by a certain age, establish a career by a certain age, purchase a house by a certain age, and so on. Once again, intent is noble coming from those guiding us, as they only want to see the best for us. Unfortunately though, it often turns time into an enemy, something dreaded and thought of often as we approach and worry about the impending deadlines.

The psychological and emotional effects can become overwhelming and overcome our thoughts, actions, and overall well-being, often to the point of severe depression, isolation, feelings of extreme failure, and suicide. The effects of not hitting the timeline or in many cases simply worrying about the upcoming timeline can throw many into a storm of emotions that often turn deadly. Clock time can and does wreak havoc on many lives—now and in the past and it certainly will in the future—as we vest significant interest and merit in honouring that which is set out in front of us by those who love us. We want to honour our guidelines, as we strive to honour those who set them.

For many, not hitting the anticipated timelines set forth by those before us can become habitual. It can actually become part of one's identity, a running joke in a family, and contribute to a great degree to one's overall sense of well-being and one's self-esteem. All too often, families talk about and share comments such as, "Someday she will grow up," "He'll never get married," and so on. Non-conformance to the best-laid plans can indeed become a psychological burden, extremely difficult to bear.

In addition to life timelines, there are so many other ways that time can be detrimental to one's well-being. So very often, many among us have our thoughts consumed by the hopes and dreams of the future. We live each day looking for salvation in tomorrow. We look for a better job, a new house, the perfect mate, the birth of a child, more money, and on and on. We tell ourselves, we convince ourselves, that when we hit our intended mark, that at this point, we will have made it and we can truly be happy. It consumes many to the point that this is all they think about, often to the point of obsession. Daily life, daily interactions with others, and daily responsibilities can suffer to varying degrees, as the hopes of tomorrow obliterate the importance of the present day.

We chase dreams, goals, and ambitions day by day into the future, and for many, the day never comes. The effects of not hitting the mark can ripple in the waters of our existence, reaching and affecting everything within us. With the accumulation of our lost dreams, our lost ambitions, we can again be driven into the plane of simple existence, whereby life consists of various shades of grey. Our psychological makeup and our inner determination and drive to succeed are paramount and necessary in our existence, and tasting success, reaching our targets, can bring a wonderful sense of accomplishment and pride to us. We need to have goals and ambitions, but in reality, they keep many minds too often projecting into the future and obliterate the most important point of time in our existence—the current moment. The current moment exposes our being to another dimension when we are alert and open to it. This is the dimension that I have spoken of earlier, the dimension unseen that is part of everyone and everything. It can be and is, our greatest asset when our awareness aligns with it. A fantastic book that delves deep into the power of the moment is *The Power of Now*, by Eckhart Tolle.

As easily and frequently as we may become projected and pinned to our future, we can also bear the weight of the chains of our past, which often leaves us treading water, struggling just to stay above the surface. Often, the weight can overcome our psychological and emotional ability to persevere, and we sink below the surface to the point of no return. Many throw in the towel for the last time and land on the plane of simple existence; others land in institutions that can help or hinder their opportunity to resurface, and many remove themselves from their earthly existence by taking their own lives. Countless individuals incessantly remind themselves and those around them what experience or situation ruined their lives, ruined their existence to the point that happiness or any real sense of peace will never be attainable. Their parents were not there for them, a relative violated them in sexual manner, everyone always picked on them, they were never smart enough in school, and so on. And yet others have one experience after another that grasps them in the hands of time. New hurts, resentments, wrongdoings, or guilt obliterates the revisiting and memories of the last and becomes the new nail in the coffin. The past experiences dissolve from consciousness but slip deep into the subconscious, stirring and building within, adding to our deep inner pain, assuredly to again resurface in a future space and time.

Time as we have come to know it, come to experience it, has one of the most destructive effects upon our overall well-being and spiritual condition, as human beings. The Moody Blues touch on the destructive nature of the past and the future with their song "The Voice," in the following line:

"With your arms around the future, and your back up against the past." [7]

Incessant recall of the past and continual projection into the future occupy our thoughts and our minds and detrimentally block the one and only point in time that matters, the current moment. The current moment is the only entry to the gates of heaven, through which we can consciously enter eternity. When we pay respect to the current moment unchained to either past or future, we can then know our immortality and know peace that is absolutely impossible to truly explain. Life as we know it is not a roll of the dice, it is not a rat race, and it is definitely not controlled by each of us, to anywhere near the extent we may think!

We often build our lives, our careers, and our families under the impression that our words, our actions, and our way of thinking has shaped and moulded ourselves and our surroundings- either successfully or unsuccessfully. We fill our heads and our egos with pride at perceived success and hold our hearts in sorrow with perceived failure. We tally the wins and losses of ourselves based on our own actions and results, and the wins and losses of others in our close circle based on our guidance, input, and direction. We take personal credit for perceived success or responsibility for perceived failure. We think we are in it alone, and we think we control all that happens to us—good, bad, or indifferent.

---

[7] Written by David Hornday, Diallo Peacock, Diawa Kanyama Peacock, Gerald Valentine • Copyright © Sony/ATV Music Publishing LLC, Universal Music Publishing Group

We do not control much of ourselves at all and even less of those and the world around us. We are not here to ride the continual roller coaster of pain and pleasure, happiness and sorrow, good and bad for nothing. We are here to experience the ride, good and bad, that ultimately reveals our true selves and that which we are all an intricate part of—Unconditional Love. We climb the ladder of life, one rung at a time, and shed the illusory layers of untruth one layer at a time. Our minds, our egos, continually replay our experiences, situations, and relationships until truth reveals itself in the crosshairs of our sight, our vision, and our lives. This is why we are here, and this is where we come to know ourselves, our brothers and sisters, and the loving Presence silently cheering us on! This is where we *know love-* and know that it is this that we have sought all along.

Time exists for this reason and this reason only. We all follow our own paths to the truth, creating and healing the wounds we both inflict and experience. Every relationship, every interaction, and every experience we encounter shuffles us through a myriad of doorways and pathways in the glorious maze of the universe, and growth in understanding and awareness awaits us through every door and around every corner. As much as we see ourselves, others, and the world itself in a state of emotional and spiritual unrest, we are all moving forward and learning Love. We may see the hate, the atrocities committed, the continual unrest and persecution in our world and point fingers and cast judgment. We may continue to create and see the wounds of the world, but all wounds eventually heal. This we will come to know in our own moment of clarity.

"Time heals all wounds, and when all wounds are healed, time as it is known ceases to exist"

Right now, as my fingers are typing this sentence, I am experiencing a group of gentlemen discussing the current state of our worldly affairs— five of them to be precise, all adding to the continued subject of ISIS and what is needed to tackle this world issue once and for all. Retaliation, force, and hate toward this movement are the prominent themes emanating from their table. Love, compassion, and understanding are unfortunately absent in any of that which is falling upon my ears. Comments from one gentleman make clear that his opinion is that there is nothing in this world that makes any sense anymore, nothing whatsoever. This conversation is taking place throughout every corner of the world, in every minute of every day. The people and subject matter may differ, but the confusion, questions, and lack of understanding and awareness thread a common bond.

Yes, it is very hurtful to see the ways of the world, to see what we do to one another in the name of freedom, religion, and the pursuit of justice, equality, and fairness, and we indeed experience the wounds of the world. We will continually experience our wounds and those of the world, until our own experiences and the grace of deep spiritual awareness touch us at our core. *This is what we live for,* and it is a destination beyond the wildest dreams anyone could ever really have!

When we are no longer a slave to psychological time, the past and the future, we lovingly and graciously arrive in the arms of eternity. We can now feel at our centre that we truly are immortal and that we are all connected to the Universal Heart, the Universal Mind. We come to know the divine importance of ourselves, of every other living being, and everything else in our universe. Our world profoundly changes from "me" to "we," and our inner awareness, our inner understanding will never be the same.

With arrival on this rung of the ladder of life, arrival of a radical new awareness is prominent. When we know, when we feel the importance of all of us in our hearts, we lovingly join the movement that *is the Universal plan*, from the beginning of time as we know it. The plan includes the soul, the spirit of all of us. It doesn't leave anyone or any soul behind. It evades and eludes completion until we guide and help one another to its fruition, to its complete realization by all contained within.

We see the love, and we see the desires and efforts of many before us to share the realization with us. Great artists, writers, musicians, world leaders, and religious figures who know the truth share it through their gifts. The gifts of art or lyrics or words are meant to strike a chord within the spirit that they may fall upon. Some of these profound influences include those such as the Buddha, Ghandi, Martin Luther King Jr., Albert Einstein, Michelangelo, Khalil Gibran, and of course Jesus, to name a few. Some recent and current prominent influences include spiritual writers and leaders Eckhart Tolle, Deepak Chopra, the late Wayne Dyer, and Marianne Williamson. They are great authors with profound potential to strike a chord with their readers and audiences. In my journey, as mentioned before, it has been the music and words of many musical groups and artists that I have experienced in my life, such as Genesis, Rush, David Bowie,

Collective Soul, Yes, the Eagles, and the Moody Blues, to name a few. I have recently been experiencing quite a bit of music from Queen and have come to know the depths and understanding of the late Freddie Mercury, in many of his profound lyrics. In the song "A Kind of Magic," he sings, with passion driven by deep understanding,

"the bell that rings inside your mind-Is challenging the doors of time"[8]

Queen display their deep understanding and awareness in many of their songs and do so out of love for all of humanity. This particular line in this song reflects exactly that of which I speak pertaining to time and our own quest for its real meaning. They share their own awareness of the world, in the knowing that their lyrics will touch the spirits of those upon the rung ready to accept and ready to understand. They share their own awareness of the world, with deep and profound gratitude to the universe, for the grace of awareness bestowed upon them.

Awareness and our position upon the ladder can often be a product of our environment or a direct result of our environment—physically, emotionally, and spiritually. As in many circumstances in the corners of the world, the basics of everyday survival elude many—food, potable water, medicine, or the medical facilities to address issues that we in North America and other developed countries take for granted. When our basic needs are unfulfilled, it is in most cases extremely difficult to move in the direction of inner well-being, although it is

---

[8] Songwriters: Roger Taylor
  A Kind Of Magic lyrics © Sony/ATV Music Publishing LLC

these paths that ultimately arrive at the door of truth in some time and space as it is known. This concept, this theory in psychology, was introduced in 1943 by Abraham Maslow and is known as Maslow's hierarchy of needs. This hierarchy contains stages of the more basic needs at the bottom of the hierarchy, moving upward, as follows:

physiological, safety, love/belonging, esteem, and self-actualization.

Maslow's belief was that in order to progress up the hierarchy of needs, one must not only achieve each level but master it. He theorized that self-actualization was the highest point of motivation and sums this up with his words, "What a man can be, he must be."

This level refers to what a person's full potential is and the realization of that potential. He later explored and revealed an expansion, a further dimension to self-actualization, which has come to be known as self-transcendence. Self-transcendence is outlined by Maslow as the self only finds its actualization in giving of itself to some higher goal outside oneself, in altruism and spirituality.

When one reaches self-actualization, self-transcendence, one's talents and gifts are realized and one paints upon the canvas of life to add depth, beauty, and understanding to our world in one way, shape, or form. Regardless of tools or materials, each is utilized to inspire others toward realizing their own gifts, their own understanding of that which lives within all of us. They long to awaken the giant that resides in us all, in the love and understanding that we will then carry out our own destiny of awakening others!

Whether it be musicians, writers, religious figures, or anyone else with knowledge of truth at their core, their gifts and their talents were bestowed upon them and they were graciously led to the awareness of their gifts to share them with the world and to move the world forward in discovery of Self. And as these figures I speak of have been bestowed a gift, there is a gift within us all that will to come to fruition and ultimately and lovingly contribute to the salvation of us all, the salvation of the Whole.

Awakening others becomes the ultimate goal, the ultimate motivation upon discovery of our true Self. There is absolutely no higher realization or reward, if you will, within our earthy existence. Love and understanding of others becomes part of our existence and part of every new experience encountered. We may not appreciate or like the words or actions of others, but we will understand why they act or speak in the manner in which they do. We may be slandered, hurt, persecuted, or ultimately misunderstood, but we hold our ground in our knowing. We hold our ground in our ultimate unity.

As we venture down the path of life, we continually learn of Self by unlearning of ourselves. Our journey takes us upon many rungs of the ladder, ultimately heading north, of course, even amid the perceived turmoil and storms that beset us. Psychological time consumes us, worries us, scares us, and many times defeats us, until we challenge its existence. When we can ultimately laugh in the face of time and know that it is not a threat, it is not our enemy, and it simply does not exist, we can then follow the call of the universe and know we are safe in its loving arms!

Chapter 7

THE UNIVERSE CALLS

The Universe Calls

Water abides in essence to rise
From river, ocean, and rill.
Up and away, painting the skies
With clouds, some shifting, some still.

Drifting in air and countless in form,
Raindrops eventually do fall.
A gentle drizzle, a tumultuous storm
Each beckoned by Universal Call.

A seedling distends through soil to air,
It's life flourishing, in rain and in sun.
With all other form it does gracefully share
In accord, and together as one.

From it's growth to destruction, to sustain other form
Surrendering life, and impartial to fall.
Consumed with reason, that only to transform,
As implored, by the Universal Call.

A grey squirrel does scurry, amid lustrous leaves
The seasons now beckoning a turn.
Rigorously burying each acorn it retrieves
With vigour, with purpose, with yearn.

Innate movement, up and down tree
Throughout branches, majestic and tall.
The creature does abide in what it can't see
The indiscernible, the Universal Call.

Cognition and emotion befall human mind
Obscuring the axiom of Being.
Separate, afraid, alone, and confined
Repercussions of misguided seeing.

To live as does Nature, impeccable and whole
Does ultimately come back to us all.
To gaze deep within, at core of One's soul
Gives resolution, to the Universal Call.

We as human beings are on top of the food chain and have the greatest ability and the highest intelligence of all living beings walking the face of the earth. This can be our greatest blessing or our greatest curse, contingent on our understanding and awareness upon the ladder of life. These characteristics bestowed upon us literally keep us in hell- or lift us up to a state of heaven on earth. Being shackled within the confines of the mind, life can strap us into the perpetual merry-go-round of well-being, and we seldom exit the wheel with any sustained inner peace. As outlined in earlier chapters, we walk through many situations, interactions, and experiences that bring us pleasure, pain, and everything in between. When intimately involved day in and day out with our egos, subconsciously we exist in a continual love/hate relationship, regardless of the superficialities that we or any others see or perceive. When we exist in a state of separation, when we see ourselves and all others individually, the universe lovingly waits in the wings for our awakening.

Yes, independence can be and is a powerful force for progression and evolution when inaugurated by leaders of love. One voice against many to move us all forward can ring the bell of time immensely. Without these spiritual stances, we collectively spin in limbo. Independence, separation, and leading only with the mind in any other circumstance are conceived in the belly of fear, and birth to serenity is postponed. Whether in our families, communities, businesses, governments, or any other collective bodies, there is no escape from this phenomenon until enough hearts join and move toward a solution, toward Love.

We continually chase the coat tails of happiness through relationships, status, material gains, and the peg on the board that puts us in an acceptable position of one-upmanship. Unfortunately when tied to the ego, we can never subconsciously place the last peg, and our minds contrive the next move to bring us to our illusory goal. We continually gaze into our mirror and the mirrors of others and strive for the next person, place, or thing that will enhance our reflection.

Our existence is so very, very simple, but we inevitably add a multitude of complexities created by our thoughts, actions, and words throughout our lives. When we are led by our minds, our separation, our egos, we evade the guidance that all other beings walking and existing upon the face of the earth follow—universal Guidance. We need only open our hearts, eyes, and minds to everything, apart from ourselves and other human beings around us, to experience the flow of life as intended.

Proof of this is all around us every minute, every day, every year. Here in Canada, most of us experience four seasons to varying degrees. Here in Ontario, we experience four delightful seasons, typically with clean, crisp lines between. With the birth of each spring, we see new life sprout and flourish, summer brings warmth and beauty to our lazy days, our forests paint the backdrops with vibrant hues upon the arrival of fall, and white backdrops and grey skies round out our frigid winters. The seasons flow into and out of one another, and nature follows its loving lead without doubt, without resistance, and without question. Abundant illustrations are apparent all around us throughout every moment in time, in every season. We witness the preparatory actions of many animals gathering and storing food in the fall months, birds and butterflies migrating to warmer climates, and trees casting aside their blanket of leaves to make way for new birth and growth in the coming spring. Winter lulls many species into a long, peaceful period of hibernation, and spring yields witness to the excitement of new life as an array of wildlife prepare for the arrival of their offspring. Nature and its loving inhabitants continually display the perpetual guidance of that unseen, each coexisting in a manner conducive to the natural order of life and each yielding to stages or circumstances beckoned by the universal call.

We also witness natural evolution in the lifeblood of our existence on earth—water and oxygen. Water molecules, changing states between a liquid, solid, and gas, move recurrently through cycles of evaporation and transpiration (evapotranspiration). The universe thoughtlessly, effortlessly transforms water through its various states in order to form clouds that birth the rain showers, feeding all plant life, which in turn provides our other human staple of existence— oxygen. In these natural occurrences, there are no debates, opinions, or resentments when one state of existence is made extinct to become yet another; the universe calls, and it is graciously answered.

The ultimate sacrifice, the ultimate death of a universal creation is that of the stars. Our universe gives birth to the stars, and after their formation and life cycle, which is said to be approximately 10 billion years for a main sequence type, they die. Their death is a result of the core exhausting its supply of hydrogen fuel, and under the weight of gravity, they contract and then expand to the point of explosion.

This sacrifice by the universe ultimately has led to the evolution of much on earth, including us as human beings! Yes, we come from the stars, and we are literally made from stardust. We must really ask ourselves, how can we not shine? In John Lennon's song "Instant Karma," he shares with us his understanding and awareness in the verse that tells us that we are all brilliant within and we do indeed shine like the moon and the stars and the sun!

Virtually every element and atom in our body is comprised of star material, other than those created during the big bang, namely hydrogen. We in fact have atoms that coexist in the formation of our bodies that are millions of years old. Does this not indicate we are a phenomenal part of our universe as human beings and as such should follow its natural order and the universal call?

Everything in existence follows the call impeccably, everything, that is, except one life force, one species—humans. We so often follow our minds and our egos into a terrain of turmoil and other times into the deep pits of despair. The Canadian rock band Rush created a profound parody in one of their great early writings and recordings, wittily outlining the problems and contempt evolving in nature, in a song titled "The Trees." The music is beautifully orchestrated, and the lyrics cleverly depict the human condition in existence for eons. An existence which includes perceived separation, injustices, collective reasoning, and collaboration. One which continually inflicts justice—to intelligently remedy whatever the circumstances warrant. The fourth line of the last verse of the song is particularly intriguing to me, in relation to the human condition. This line states that the one species of trees will force another to give them light. Intriguing indeed, as it is light, it is Love, that all subconsciously seek.

> **So the maples formed a union**
> **And demanded equal rights**
> **'The oaks are just too greedy**
> **We will make them give us light'**
> **Now there's no more oak oppression**
> **For they passed a noble law**
> **And the trees are all kept equal**
> **By hatchet, axe, and saw** [9]

We cannot demand or ask light from anyone or anything, but when aligned with our minds, our human egoic condition, we continually look outside ourselves and to others for justice, happiness, freedom, and light. We search the four corners of the earth, leaving no stone unturned, until such time as we turn the stone of self. It is then and only then that we begin to understand our real source of Light.

Our human condition when mandated by the mind insidiously clutches us in the realms of illusion and barricades the gates of freedom. Freedom is only possible, only attainable, when our own choices bring us to the Gatekeeper, and the Gatekeeper lovingly grants us entry. These choices we have come to know as free will.

---

[9] Songwriters: Geddy Lee / Alex Lifeson / Neil Peart
The Trees lyrics © Sony/ATV Music Publishing LLC, Ole MM, Ole Media Management Lp

In the *Meriam-Webster* dictionary, *free will* is defined in the following way:

1. voluntary choice or decision
2. freedom of humans to make choices that are not determined by prior causes or by divine intervention (meriam websters learners dictionary)

Free will is the indescribable gift bestowed upon our species to ultimately bring us back into the loving arms of God, our brothers and sisters, and eternity. Free will is the universal gift that indelibly displays true, unconditional love. It remains our greatest blessing, as it is our key to unlocking the doors of time, one experience at a time.

As glorious as it is in reality, it is also our archenemy with the most significant impact and devastation upon our state of well-being. When we make choices that hurt us, or any other for that matter, there are emotional and spiritual consequences, such as inner turmoil, anxiety, guilt, and unhappiness. These consequences are experienced on a regular basis or intermittently but are subconsciously inescapable or undeniable in times of our illusive deception; they hold us in psychological time.

"Free-will is the gift of choice granted to each and all. When choices are made that are not in line with natural law, simultaneously the law of cause and effect is initiated. The cumulative effect that we experience, ultimately leads to future choice aligned with natural law. We must therefore ask ourselves, does free-will truly exist in the absence of time?"

When we can no longer tolerate, accept, or live with choices that stir our undesirable pot of pain, we are lovingly led to new levels of awareness, whereby we can feel the pull and hear the soft whisper of our most precious gift—the gift, the voice, the universal call that silently, lovingly nudges us to choose again, in the instances and experiences in which choice is misaligned with natural law.

As we accumulate and acquire every new situation or experience under our belts of being, our choices move us up and down a myriad of rungs, up and down many paths, and through the emotions, feelings, and sensations experienced with each. It is frequently observed and experienced that we can literally bang our heads against the wall of deception over and over again, thinking that the next blow will be the last. We irrefutably take one more kick at the can and hope we will hit the sweet spot and bring ourselves to the point of whatever satisfaction or desired result we so desperately seek. We inevitably partake in this behavioural manner in our relationships, desires, actions, words, and life in general.

Our willing participation in these behaviours becomes our only means of shedding illusion and unlearning that which has become ingrained in our psyche. Free will can take us into places that often shock or confuse those in our circle, leaving them wondering what we are thinking, experiencing, or what planet we are coming from! We ask ourselves the same questions when witnessing others' actions, thoughts, or lifestyles. Why can't they just keep quiet at social events? When are they going to grow up and take some responsibility? Don't they know how to keep a husband, wife, or partner? Free will takes all of us in directions that are questioned by both ourselves and others at times, with choices or decisions that may appear negative and also choices that may appear positive.

To elaborate, we may choose a prestigious career that we ourselves and others in our circle deem worthy, noble, and prosperous. Free will leads us through an education, entry into our chosen field, a general learning curve to learn the ropes of our endeavour, and then arrival in whole to our chosen destination. We may in fact reap great financial rewards or gain status that provides us and those around us a sense of pride in our accomplishments. When aligned with our internal need to know ourselves, we can evolve and find great satisfaction and a sense of well-being. Life can evolve and provide all we need to place us upon our intended rung. But when this choice is not bringing what we need to learn and remember to the surface, no matter how great the financial rewards or positional ranking, there will be a gentle calling or a boisterous shout for change from the universe itself. We cannot escape our intended spiritual growth in our existence, no matter how the situation may appear on the surface. Free will takes us where we want to consciously go, and the universe is there to whisper or shout or shake us to our next point or destination in self-discovery when our choices, decisions, and courses of action are misaligned.

I witnessed this first-hand just recently, as this past weekend, after dropping our daughter off for a venture to Italy with her school, my wife and I went to a club in Toronto to see a musician, Trevor Hall, whom my wife and I have come to appreciate. His music is very spiritually inspiring, and he is indeed blessed, talented, and sharing his gifts with the world as beckoned by the universal call. He is definitely fighting the good fight! The opening act was a gentleman in his early thirties, and upon starting his performance, he shared with the audience his journey that brought him to the stage that night. He shared that a few years prior, when working in a large law firm in Toronto, he questioned all that he was doing, what he stood for, and why he was doing it. He actually stated that he felt that he would be selling his soul to continue on the path he had then trod upon. He experienced the universe calling him to go out on a limb, take a chance and a leap of faith, and follow a new path to a new destination. He accommodated the calling, expressed his heartfelt gratitude for the leap he undertook, and touched all those in the audience with a wonderfully inspiring performance that struck the hearts of many.

Free will takes us in and out of many experiences, both positive and negative, and ultimately we settle into the arms of satisfaction or the grip of unhappiness with each experience, interaction, or life situation. There is no escaping the gentle whispers or the aggressive shouts of the universe; we are continually acquainted with the direction to follow, and our subsequent choices land us at the next point of calling.

Resistance is futile, as no matter where we step, walk, or run, we can never escape the call within. Yes, we can find temporary shelter or temporary relief through new environments, relationships, or life situations. Or we can deny the call and stay in the environment, relationship, or life situation in which we reside. Either way, we cannot escape or stay in our experience; we catch up with ourselves, or our experience continually plays upon our being, until we face, and move through that which we are called to do. Resistance will lead us to further discontent, emotional turmoil, or even physical pain or ailments. Many among us do remain in a living hell, sometimes until we no longer walk the face of the earth, but as it is eternity, there will be a point in time all rise above the hell that keeps us down. Again, resistance is futile; the call to evolve and grow is undeniable to us as humans, as it is to all other life.

We are to live as does nature, impeccable and whole. The last verse in the poem "The Universe Calls" outlines our return to our natural state and our awareness and awakening of that which has eluded us in the restless sleep we have experienced from days long past. The *Merriam-Webster* dictionary defines *impeccable* in the following way:

1. not capable of sinning or liable to sin
2. free from fault or blame: flawless

A return to this state opposes literally everything we are told and taught in our youth in our impressionable years by our parents, teachers, and others of influence, others who came before us. This also includes many religious factions that adamantly believe and profess that God eternally remains upon his throne of judgment and delivers resolution and wrath accordingly.

Free from fault is a concept virtually impossible to believe, much less buy into and know at our core. In our prevalent perception, we all make mistakes and fault ourselves and others on a continual basis throughout our lives, to one degree or another. And it is precisely this that holds us in varying depths, varying degrees of despair, guilt, and ultimately unhappiness. We cannot and do not measure up to the perfection professed and anticipated by those who came before us, much less our creator himself.

As all is perfect within nature, how can we experience such an immense deviation in perfection ourselves as human beings? How can we be so far from that which our creator would have us be? This is the conundrum that has resonated through all of time and the state that we have come to know as common ground in our human existence. We are challenged throughout our lives as to why we did not do this or that correctly, why we behaved in a certain manner, or how we could participate in such an action. And ultimately, ironically, we are challenged and questioned by those who participate in behaviours or manners that miss the mark of perceived perfection themselves!

We see and experience day after day, year after year, blatant examples of this with news of misdoings, crimes, and atrocities committed by those within government and religious factions, authority figures, and families. We are either all guilty, sinful, and imperfect in our existence, or we are not. And ultimately, we are not! This concept needs utmost reflection, and I would encourage rereading this and the preceding paragraph once again, with reflection upon completion.

We are what we are, and we do what we do, one experience at a time, to come to know that we are perfect! Each and every one of us! Yes, we all act, speak, and participate in behaviours that are deemed inappropriate, cruel, callous, vengeful, spiteful, and so on but do so under natural order, under the guidance and loving spirit of the universal call. Every person, every individual, does the absolute best he or she can, with the resources, understanding, and awareness he or she possesses at absolutely every point, every moment of existence in the flesh. We evolve exactly as intended and grow in awareness, understanding, and ultimately love, with each subsequent interaction and experience with life.

Through experience and grace, our state of perfection is one that can and does come to the forefront of awareness in our evolution and journey of self-discovery. It is the rung of realization that changes our internal vision and understanding 180 degrees. Concurrent with this realization, forgiveness of ourselves and all others comes to light, and we can move forward wiping the sleep from our eyes in moments that we may lose ourselves momentarily in time and in experiences where we experience fear or attack and lose sight of Love.

Our awareness of this state of perfection does not sanction subsequent, continual interactions and behaviours in which we demonstrate fear or attack; we cannot rest on these laurels. Lovingly, gratefully, nor do we want to! We can now step impeccably forward one interaction, experience, and moment at a time with love in our hearts and understanding in being.

The last line of the poem encapsulating this chapter also contains the word we have come to know in the English language as *whole*. The *Merriam-Webster* dictionary defines whole as:

> (1) free of wound or injury: unhurt (2) recovered from a wound or injury: restored (3) being healed, mentally or emotionally sound ... (6) constituting the entirety of a person's nature or development

These components of the definition of the word *whole* are in the context associated with its meaning contained in the poem.

To become whole, we need to transpose our thinking toward our own and all others' impeccability. To become whole, we must also transcend our thinking and awareness beyond separation and individuality and know that we are all an important, integral part of the entire human race, the entire universe, and the entire cosmos themselves. We are One!

Chapter 8

ONE

One

A branch, leaf, a pebble
The moon and the sun,
A man, woman, child
With Life all are One.

Of age, young or old
Of skin, dark or light,
Perpetual illusion
Doth mask perfect sight.

Seeing with the senses
Impeding what is real,
Unparalleled in purpose
Is that, but to conceal.

Vision abandoning way
Albeit slowly, to Truth-
Radiant the surroundings
When born to Infinite youth.

Solid walls do but crumble
By wayside, and to the ground,
Pathways glowing luminous
Unfeigned treasure has been found.

Flowing with the river
Flourishing in the sun
A man, woman, child
With Life all are One.

In the preceding chapter, the last verse of the poem "The Universe Calls" accentuates our transcendence to becoming impeccable and whole. We reviewed the definition of the word *whole* as an adjective; we will now look at its definition as a noun. The *Merriam-Webster* dictionary defines *whole* as a noun as:

> 1: a complete amount or sum: a number, aggregate, or totality lacking no part, member, or element

> 2: something constituting a complex unity: a coherent system or organization of parts fitting or working together as one

Our entire existence—all that has been, all that is, and all that will come to be—is described with precision in this definition. In the first part of the definition, the inclusion of every part, every member, and every element is paramount and encompasses everything and everyone in our universe. It is the sovereign destination of truth, awareness, and understanding that all paths imminently lead to, for each and every one of us. It is the rung of reality in our intended climb up the ladder of life upon earth. In *The Essential Rumi* translations by Coleman Barks, the poem "The Worm's Waking" outlines our totality:

> There's a worm addicted to eating grape leaves
> Suddenly, he wakes up,
> call it grace, whatever, something
> wakes him, and he's no longer a worm.

He's the entire vineyard,

And the orchard, too, the fruit, the trunks,

A growing wisdom and joy

that doesn't need to devour.

So often we hear that we are one, so often we hear we are all children of God, or the universe or an entire brotherhood. It is apparent we have the concept as a species, but our continual words, actions, and behaviours contest this both individually and collectively. We interact with others on a daily basis, and disagreements resulting in harsh words, thoughts, and actions are prominent. When we have established our own position, opinion, or desired outcome on any subject matter or situation, our words, thoughts, and actions coincide in either a positive or negative manner. When in agreement or correlation with another's opinion or stance, we can feel a common bond and can sense our camaraderie. On the flipside, when we do not see eye to eye, we experience a sense of unease, distance, and ultimately separation, a sense and feeling that can linger and fester for long periods of time, as we often live in the here and now, with our thoughts stuck in our past. We not only see space between us, we feel it as well, and it is our primal state in our human existence.

This primal state, this perceived separation, can and does occur on an individual and collective basis and arises even within collective groups that stand for the same purpose. Delve into the inner workings and relationships in any political group, company, or other organization, and strife, competition, jealousy, and many other forms of ill feelings will surface. Within a company, there can be a sense of tension between departments, shifts, and every other possibility imaginable. Pertaining to managerial or leadership roles, clawing and fighting one's way up the corporate ladder is commonplace. Within a political group, some will side and agree with the opinions and positions of one or more members, while others remain steadfast to the intended direction or stance of others. We never escape this perpetual occurrence; it casts its shadow to varying degrees in every collective body at some point and time, as the mind, the ego, puts demands on each and every collective participant in one way, shape, or form. On an individual basis, we can experience several situations day in and day out in which we hit an emotional impasse with others, including simple events and interactions, such as someone unknowingly cutting us off while driving on a highway as his or her preoccupation with the condition of a loved one just injured in an accident is at the forefront of his or her attention. We also experience not so simple events or interactions such as a family quarrel- when we hold our position steadfast with loved ones, as we so often do.

Our primal state of existence, that of separation, rears its ugly head on a continual basis. And ironically, the typical means to resolve our separation extends our separation further. Collectively, the majority of our answers and solutions to strife, unrest, and attack is counterattack. We beget violence for violence and attack for attack with this an eye-for-an-eye mentality, and never address the core issue. The core issue always, always centres on human relations, either individually or collectively, and always centres on fear, hurt, and some form of spiritual depravation.

Our current answer to the violence, terrorism, and all other forms of attack we are experiencing in this day and age is counterattack. We typically grapple to learn from each incident and prepare and plan for comparable, future events. We are reactive for the most part, as we really never know what any individual or group is capable of. Yes, we try to stay one step ahead, but one must ask oneself, "Is this actually conceivable?" There is a world of possibilities to inflict terror, pain, and unrest, and realistically, we can never really prepare for each and every one. We initiate new security checks, policies, regulations, and whatever else necessary to combat that which has threatened or inflicted ill will or hurt upon us. These typically come with astronomical price tags. The tail wags the dog, as the dog scurries to gain control. There are several movements, organizations, and political bodies working toward peaceful resolve, but transcendence in this manner must come to the forefront, not bring up the rear.

A recent event in the United States brings this reality to the forefront, in many, many ways. A very short time ago, a young man entered a church in the Southern United States and proceeded to open fire and kill several members and the minister of the church. This terrible tragedy contains several facets of our individual and collective unrest and our means and tactics toward resolve. The young man spent an hour in Bible study and then opened fire on the attending parishioners, in what has been labelled as a hate crime. The young man fled the scene, the manhunt was on, and it wasn't long before he was brought in to police custody and charged with the nine counts of murder. Shortly thereafter, the focus went to race relations, gun violence, and arms control, commandeering many national news programs for quite some time.

Just a few days ago, the story took another turn, as news reports noted that there was an error in the system, a breakdown in the background check, and the young man would not have been able to purchase the weapons utilized had the error not occurred. We see breakdown in unity with the young man bent on inflicting his own wrath and justice. We also discern conflict and unrest as to the right to bear arms and the laws and stipulations of ownership and then target human error as a large contributing factor of this ill-fated incident, as the young man should not have been permitted to purchase the weapons. We see numerous contributing factors to this incident and also see that even with checks and measures in place, things still happen. We cannot prepare for every possible act of violence or cover and carry out all the preparations instilled or initiated. Collectively, we are not getting to the heart of the matter, and it is this that must be addressed to resolve our perpetual myriad of differences.

Where does this leave us? How do we transcend this unrest, violence, and terror? How do we reduce or eliminate the thoughts that come into our minds as to what might or will happen next? There is an encouraging outcome in the event just outlined, as many family members and church parishioners spoke out immediately to the world, proclaiming their forgiveness for the young man, a direct reflection that they possess within their hearts the brother- and sisterhood of humanity, even toward one who took the lives of several of their own. This is the course of action required to transcend the violence, atrocities, and suppression of groups, cultures, and races that arise throughout the world. It is simply love for one another as a race and understanding and awareness at our core that we are all part of the one universal heart and universal mind.

We have touched on our perceived division quite extensively thus far, with the ego predominately invoking our illusory separation, both individually and collectively. This primal state of existence paradoxically breaks us down to ultimately build us up! We can strive for and achieve tremendous feats of accomplishment, but until there is recognition and awareness of the Whole, we both risk and experience plights of pain, emotional turmoil, and other forms of individual and collective downfall. But also, as outlined in previous chapters, it is when we shed the layers of illusion, many times through pain and always through experience, that we transcend from a me to we state of mind. We transcend from mind and ego domination to heart and Being domination. We arrive on rung number One on the ladder of life!

One, the first and only number in all we have come to know, between two and infinity, with any true sustenance or reality. For practical purposes, all other numbers are needed, for finance, mathematical calculations, measurements, and the like, but in our higher awareness and in spirit, One is all that we need to understand. One- in this context, is divisible by each and every person walking the face of the earth, and all those that walked before us. One is the sum, the total of all humanity, and the only equation we need master in life as we know it.

"The Divine sum off all humanity equals One"

Upon awareness of this equation, upon knowing its true authenticity at our core, we have awoken and can now wipe the remaining sleep from the corners of our eyes! We can now look at our own reflection in the mirror of life and see our totality, and look at all others and see theirs as well. We see everyone in ourselves and ourselves in everyone; we see One, and more so we feel One! Everything in existence is divinely intertwined, divinely connected, divinely loved. This inner knowing can be felt and experienced to different degrees, but transcending the mind and the ego to the point of no return in our individuality and separation is absolutely compulsory. The mind, the ego, may sneak random thoughts of separation into our existence from time to time, but we have ultimately crossed the bridge of separation over the waters of despair into the loving, awaiting arms of Eternity. Love has conquered our minds and our egos through our experiences and through grace from the Universal heart itself. It is unquestionably the peace that passes all understanding!

The ultimate target of our existence in the flesh, for each and every one of us, is to realize our part of the Whole at the core of our being. And as mentioned, many among us profess this knowledge, but do not know it intimately within our hearts. As an example, we all know the golden rule: "Do unto others as you would have them do unto you." It is something we hear from our early years throughout our lives. It becomes ingrained within us, but how often do we truthfully conform? If we do conform, then being degraded, lied to, cheated, made fun of, or criticized is something we want for ourselves, as the majority among us partake in this type of behaviour in our lives to one degree or another. Similarly, we are taught what is right and what is wrong in our youth, as an example in the Christian religion, the 10 Commandments. Again, we know them from a young age, but conformance is never 100 percent, as we have lost ourselves in our own individuality and separation from the Whole.

When we know our part in the big scheme of things, really know it at our core, the golden rule and principles of right and wrong can be fully understood. We can now appreciate fully that doing unto others is doing onto ourselves, as we are one and the same! We are one cell in the earthly body, just as each cell in our own physical bodies miraculously coexists with others to allow our own life, our own functionality. With this intimate knowledge, coexistence, love for all others is paramount and our only way out or through the despair, hurt, and separation that is part of our world today. John Lennon captures the essence of our unity and the blocks we have experienced thus far in our existence in his song "Imagine."

> **You may say that I'm a dreamer**
> **But I'm not the only one**
> **I hope some day you'll join us**
> **And the world will be as one** [10]

---

[10] Songwriters
JOHN LENNON
Published by

John knew in his heart, at the core of his being, the importance of our unity and was awakened to the rung of understanding, which we are all destined to arrive upon. This is the perfect time to locate the words of this song and reflect on each and every one of them!

Through this awareness, through this most phenomenal experience and feeling of collective unity, we can dispel the multitude of questions and feelings experienced that held us captive in chaos and held us continually speculating why things happened to us as they did. We can cast aside the psychological burdens of the ego and know that we are perfect in our current moment, in our current awareness. We also comprehend that all those around us, all those walking the face of the earth, exist in perfection in this current moment and their current awareness as well. No good or bad, no right or wrong—*there just is.*

Also through our awareness, coincidences no longer exist, and we now comprehend that they never did. An experience that had me grinning from ear to ear and beaming with joy within occurred in my own life a short time ago. I had been shopping for some new work attire, and as I browsed throughout the men's section, a young man about eighteen years of age entered the department with a young female friend and proceeded to request assistance from the staff to put together an entire ensemble for an event that night, with a budget not to exceed 100 dollars. Three staff members diligently scurried throughout the department, each selecting appropriate shirts, pants, and ties that would work well together and fall within the young man's budget. As the young man was in the change room, trying on some of the articles, and I was within earshot, he joyously sang, "God is on my side," in a version and tune foreign to my ear. The young woman asked him to tone down, as others outside might hear. Upon hearing her request to the young man, I responded, "Hey, no worries. He is on my side too!"

A few minutes later, I was retrieving a few shirts that were close to the cash register area and noticed the lad was in a bit of a predicament. He stated he was $9.96 short of the total to purchase all the pieces of the ensemble created with the assistance of the three staff members. I immediately remembered I had one ten-dollar bill in my wallet and proceeded to quietly slip the youngster the bill, so he could be on his way to the event he seemed so eager to attend. He gratefully accepted and went on his way, thanking me several times with words and with the expression on his face. The young man had told the staff what had transpired while I had gone to try on the shirts, and they offered kind, heartfelt words at my desire to help the young man out. But you see, what I experienced was genuine care and concern for this young man by these women as they eagerly, diligently put his ensemble together. Their kindness struck a chord within me, and I, in turn, followed with the next act of kindness. I know now this is what makes the world go around; this is how we all change the world!

The story doesn't end there; this is where it gets unfathomably interesting! This is where the notion of coincidence gets thrown right out the window. This is where my awareness of our unity and a Life force beyond comprehension touched my heartstrings. My next stop was to an electronics store right next to the department store I had just left, to purchase an external backup hard drive for my daughter's laptop computer. Upon entering the store, I came across a familiar brand that happened to be on sale, and there were a couple items for different operating systems. I took one of the boxes to the sales and service counter to enquire as to the suitability for my daughter's computer. The young sales associate stated the item I had was suitable for my application but would need formatting to utilize with the operating system of the computer. He said he thought he had one specific to the system needed and proceeded to go into the back to retrieve it.

I ensued to put the box back on the shelf, and as he walked out from the back of the service area, he asked me the cost of the unit I had previously showed him. I told him it was $89.95, and he scanned the unit he had procured from the back. He then stated, "This is $99.95, but I am going to give it to you for the same price as the other."

My immediate reaction was to look up in the direction of the ceiling, smile, and thank the Universe. For what, at that moment, I did not know. I was joyously perplexed, beyond anything I had ever experienced. When I returned to my car, it was then that my gratitude really hit home, and I could fathom the depth of the experience I had just encountered. This was no chance occurrence; this was the Universe telling me, shouting to me, that the real forces in my life were those unseen, those that happen within the lives of all of us, throughout our lives—those occurrences that we have come to know as coincidence! We often say ourselves and hear others say so very often, "Oh, what a coincidence." This type of occurrence is commonplace, but the true nature and true source of such an experience had eluded me until that which I had experienced this day. It was something I will never forget and really cannot prove, but I know at the depths of my Being what occurred.

It is when we climb onto the rung of unity that we recognize coincidences for what they truly are. Here, we know the intricacies and miracles of our universe occur on a continual basis, and all events and interactions throughout are interconnected, in a synchronistic manner. This is the universe at its finest, perpetually guided by the Master computer! This is our lifeblood that we come to know intimately and transcend from reliance on ourselves to reliance on Unity! Arrival on this rung of awareness is not a question of us recognizing, only a question of what moment in eternity it will occur, for each and every one of us.

The coincidences and the synchronistic workings of our world, our existence, are attributed to one thing and one thing only—the Universal Heart and Universal Mind. Our progress and evolution as a species and the progress and evolution of our entire universe are miraculously linked to this Source. Advancement in any facet of our existence, whether it be technical, spiritual, or moral, is the result of grace from the Source, as so many who are with us today and have come before us have come to know.

Technically, many great inventors and pillars of human evolution have attested to the source of their breakthroughs not being from the confines of their own minds but coming from a field, an energy that defies explanation. Many great inventors profess that their ideas arrived while they were sleeping or dreaming and arrived into their consciousness during a void in their cognitive state. Some incredible advancements have been attributed to ideas coming in dreams. Notably, James Watson, the co-discoverer of the structure of DNA, has made the claim that he stumbled upon the double helix image for the DNA chain through his dream of a spiral staircase. Other breakthroughs of this nature include the sewing machine, which came in a dream to inventor Elias Howe, and Descartes's new science philosophy was discovered in a dream he encountered on November 10, 1619. The discovery of benzene is a direct result of a dream experienced by Friedrich August Kekule von Stadonitz, who saw a group of snakes swallowing their tails.

We can also recognize a multitude of other creative works that evolved from dreams, such as great books and music. Mary Shelley, author of *Frankenstein*, saw a pale student kneeling beside the thing he had put together and then saw the hideous phantasm of a man stretched out and with some powerful internal working engine show signs of life. James Cameron, creator of many modern books and movies, professes *The Terminator* was linked to a dream. Stephanie Meyer, the creator of the Twilight saga, also cites a dream as the source for her idea. Many great songs came to fruition through dreams. Paul McCartney dreamed the melody to the song "Yesterday," and the guitar riff by Keith Richards in the song "(I Can't Get No) Satisfaction" came about while he was fast asleep.

As in actual or lucid dreams, we also experience scientific, technical, and other progressive breakthroughs for humanity on a continual basis during our waking moments, which we will explore in greater detail in the next chapter. These breakthroughs combat new viral strains or technical obstructions that hold us back in our evolution or inspire peace movements that work toward resolving years, decades, or centuries of hurt. We have seen that no matter what is presented to us as a species, we work for resolution in time and successfully for the most part. We can look at many illnesses or diseases that have plagued humankind and see solutions—smallpox, malaria, and AIDS, to name a few. Technologically, we have seen the evolution in the latter part of the twentieth century that has catapulted us into the twenty-first century. And in race relations, although still strained throughout the world to a certain degree, we know how far we have come since the fifties and sixties with our evolution in North America. We are continually advancing with individuals and collective bodies connecting to the Source, and God only knows what is yet to come!

One of my favourite songs in existence is by the band Genesis, and its title says it all, "Watcher of the Skies." It has intrigued me for many years, and one verse speaks directly to our unity as a species, as a universe. Genesis points out in the first line of this verse that our life realization, our reality, turns from a point of singularity to one of unity, or oneness. Upon coming to this realization, upon awakening, our journey is not complete. They go on to say—and beautifully I might add—that although we have our feet firmly planted in understanding, the storms of life will continue and then inquire as to our ability to remain afloat on the "ocean of Being." This song and these lyrics show the depth, awareness, and understanding of these young musicians, as they were in their early twenties when this song headlined their 1972 Album *Foxtrot*.

From life alone to life as one,

Think not now your journey's done

For though your ship be sturdy, no

Mercy has the sea,

Will you survive on the ocean of being?[11]

The last two lines of this song finish the song in a phenomenally profound fashion. The second-to-last line outlines the Watcher of all, the heartbeat and intelligence, the Universal Heart and Universal Mind. The last line outlines the fate of our universe to the watcher Himself. But as the watcher of all, we are Him, and He is us. God lives in each and every one of us. This is our one fate, and this fate is our own! Source the words to this song, and reflect on the wisdom contained!

The word *one* and *won* are two different words with two different meanings. But upon the rung of awareness, which we are destined to reach, they coalesce together in a most fascinating and stunning manner and create an altogether new word and new meaning. The word is *"Wone"*, and simply put, it means, "When we know we are

---

[11] Written by Anthony Banks, Michael Rutherford, Peter Gabriel, Phil Collins, Steven Hackett • Copyright © Sony/ATV Music Publishing LLC, Warner/ Chappell Music, Inc

One, we have won." We have won our place on the rung of awareness through our experiences and won the long, insidious battle with our greatest enemy, our ego. We have been awakened to the awareness of Unity, and found the place in both our heart and soul that lead us to truly understanding ourselves, all our brothers and sisters, and our essential existence in the human race. Grace has been bestowed upon us beyond our wildest dreams, and we have been touched upon our heartstrings in a manner in which we will never be the same again!

Chapter 9

HEARTSTRINGS

Heartstrings

Angelic voices singing, a child's first word,
A vision, a memory, among things.
Subtle sensations, those felt, not heard,
Ethereal touch, upon the heartstrings.

A tingling sensation invades the present moment
Appearing without ending or start.
Quiet is mind, internally silent
Tenderly strummed, the strings of the heart.

Resonant vibrations at core of essence,
The prodigious feeling it brings.
Words can't describe in form of sentence,
The music played, upon the heartstrings.

Truth be felt in but a twinkling of time-

A feeling which one can't impart.

Momentary heaven, a state of sublime

When echo the strings of the heart.

Journey forward in faith, journey forward with love,

Journey forward, being open to all things,

The moment awaits, when touched from above-

Upon the Divine, the golden heartstrings.

Heartstrings are the strings within our Being, that are lovingly touched, lovingly played upon by life itself, lovingly strummed in times of experiencing bliss, experiencing a moment of pure joy. The world stops for but a moment, and we experience the feeling of eternity and the feeling of Love at our core. For myself, it usually leads to a feeling that encompasses my entire body, and goose bumps send the hair on my arms straight up toward the heavens! It's really quite spectacular, and all I can do is smile and thank life itself upon each occurrence.

For many, our hearts are touched on special occasions, special events, or times of great significance within our lives, key times within our lives, such as during the union of marriage, the birth of a child, or any other event that we come to cherish and define as a highlight in our existence. We can experience the feeling of joy and bliss and very often recapture the feeling at a future moment in time by simply arousing the memory.

I can reflect on many highlights within my own life and have a tremendous sense of joy encapsulate my being for that moment, such as learning of my wife's pregnancies. When I learned of the coming arrival of my first daughter, Ashley, my wife and I weathered a tremendous blizzard to go to our parents, as we were uncontrollably compelled to share the joy with others within the family. We encountered a blizzard one would not normally even drive in, but my excitement and joy overcame any fear and common sense that told me to wait for a better time. Off we went to share our fantastic news, and sleep was not scheduled to arrive for me that entire night! I experienced similar

Climbing Life's Eternal Ladder

feelings of joy with the news of our second arrival, Alyssa, as well, at the thought of my beautiful, loving wife bringing life to yet another bundle of joy! There is definitely a reason babies are called a "bundle of joy," and I have been blessed to experience this first-hand!

Another personal experience I encountered within my family occurred when I required surgery at about the age of 30. The experience of the surgery was not welcome or did not bring joy, but something truly magical, truly eye opening did result, that did bring joy and sense of awe to me after the fact. After my surgery I developed an extremely high fever, and the night that it developed, my daughter Ashley who was about two years old at the time awoke my wife Lisa during a dream she experienced. She relayed to my wife that "daddy burning, daddy hot". My wife consoled her, and got her back to sleep.

The next day my wife arrived to visit me, unaware of my fever that had developed the night before. As we spoke and she learned of what had occurred, she relayed to me the dream our daughter Ashley had, and we both were amazed at what had transpired, but both knew deep within that this was no coincidence, no chance dream under the circumstances. Today, when remembering this experience, I truly have a sense of joy- joy of the connectedness to my daughter, and joy to the understanding of connectedness to the Universal Mind, of which we are all connected.

There have been many other key moments that have occurred within my life. Another I can reflect upon this very moment, as I sit writing and remembering my wedding day and the friends and family who made the time and the memories so special. Currently, I am on an ATV trip with my wife, Lisa, and three of my lifelong friends and their spouses at an ATV camp in the Haliburton/Muskoka area of Ontario. A couple of these guys strummed the heartstrings of life within me on my wedding day, when they cleverly and lovingly created and performed a song with my other groomsman. I can reflect and remember as if it were yesterday how proud I was of my beautiful wife and the fantastic friends who put the song together to share on our special day. To you guys, I thank you forever! We all have these defining moments within our lives, moments that touch us in a way that stays with us, many times for the duration of our existence, times that strike a fire within our hearts and curl the corners of our mouths toward the skies, times that generate a genuine feeling that it is great to be alive!

We can also experience the pull on our heartstrings in our everyday lives, in everyday occurrences, in times that one might consider uneventful. In reality, they are phenomenally eventful, phenomenally important in our upward climb on the rungs of awareness, the rungs of our awakening. These are experiences when time stands still and we are touched on our heartstrings to momentarily feel the existence within us that longs to surface and brilliantly shine! In these times, we are internally silent long enough to have the strings of our hearts strummed and the light of life to shine upon our awareness in but a twinkling of time.

As I said earlier, music has been a huge inspiration to me and has touched my heartstrings many, many times when I least expected it.

I have always listened to and loved the music of the late 1960s and early 1970s, mainly progressive rock, including bands such as Yes, Genesis, the Moody Blues, and Canada's own power rock trio Rush, to name a few. There have been some later bands that have touched my being, such as Talking Heads in the 1980s and Collective Soul in the 1990s, but the main influence on my awareness came to fruition with the older works. I have included many of the lyrical themes of songs in this book, in direct relation to the ideas and points of awareness I am attempting to bring to the forefront. As highlighted in chapter 6, "Of Time and Oneself," musicians, artists, poets, and the like have lovingly shared their awareness and gratitude to life itself through their works, in their own calling from life, to touch others on their golden heartstrings! In reference to musicians, their instrumentation and composition of music is indeed spectacular, but if we listen closely to the lyrics, we can hear the call to come home, the call to awaken.

Over the years, this philosophical music has evolved for me, as my eyes have slowly opened. I have always enjoyed the musical composition and the intricate ways these bands brought each of their individual talents together so tightly to form the music. Each instrument, each note and chord, melds together in perfect unison to soothe my ears and quiet my heart! On the album *Foxtrot* by Genesis, "Can Utility and the Coast Liners" commands each and every hair on my arms to full attention in a portion where Steve Hackett's acoustic guitar answers Tony Banks's power chords on the keyboards. Powerful stuff indeed!

As my awareness has grown through my life experiences and through continuity in listening to this most intriguing music, the lyrics have continued to launch themselves out of the speakers and land upon my heartstrings. Many of these artists express their deep understanding of our unity, love, and life itself in the majority of their works. The Canadian band Rush have done this throughout their phenomenal career, especially in their earlier works with songs, such as "Closer to the Heart," "Trees," and "Something for Nothing." They have brought about continuity in their message later in the 1980s and beyond with songs, such as "Tom Sawyer," "Time Stand Still," and "New World Man," to name but a few. In the earlier song, "Something for Nothing," Rush emphasizes in the chorus the dream state in which we exist and our evolution toward awakening, toward freedom. They relay to us that freedom isn't free, and I relate this to us going through trials and tribulations to attain freedom, one experience at a time.

Oh you don't get something for nothing
You don't get freedom for free
You won't get wise
With the sleep still in your eyes
No matter what your dreams might be [12]

In their song "New World Man," included in their 1982 album *Signals*, they emphasize our growth and awareness through our evolution one experience at a time or, as they put it, one mistake and one mess at a time!

The Moody Blues have also blessed us with beautifully written

---

[12] Songwriters: Gary Lee Weinrib / Neil Elwood Peart
Something for Nothing lyrics © Sony/ATV Music Publishing LLC, Ole MM, Ole Media Management Lp

music and lyrics throughout their careers, with older songs, such as "Isn't Life Strange." I especially admire the verse that tells us life is a book without light, unless it is one written with love—phenomenal! In later works, on their 1983 album *The Present*, they outline the state of awakening beautifully in their song "Blue World." The very first line highlights the heart and soul taking control—awakening!

As I have listened to these and many other songs and artists for several years now, they have always intrigued me and drawn me back to listen again and again. Through time and through life, one experience at a time, all of these songs have been a part of my journey, and with each new listening experience, I now hear with a new set of ears what they are saying, and I now feel within my heartstrings the message these artists are trying to convey. All I can say is "Thank you all, from the bottom of my heart, for sharing your awareness and love for all within your songs."

As we can be touched on our heartstrings by music, as I have been, we can also be touched by great literary works of poetry, philosophy, and the like. I have read many great inspirational writings by new age authors, such as Eckhart Tolle, Marianne Williamson, and the late Wayne Dyer, to name a few. And I have also experienced the profound writing by the Foundation for Inner Peace in the book *A Course in Miracles* that all of the aforementioned authors refer to in their writings as well. This was a most intriguing book and was a huge part of my evolution, as was its intent. This is one read that drills to the core of our spiritual confusion, our perceived illusion, and the means to rectify how we see ourselves, others, and the world we live in. It really can touch the heartstrings of our existence and allow us to experience miracles in our everyday human experience. Another book that has had a deep impact on my evolution was published in 1923 by Lebanese artist, philosopher, and author Kahlil Gibran, entitled *The Prophet.* This book was written as 26 prose poetry essays combined with various drawings from the author himself and is a phenomenal read that can aid our continual transcendence.

Life has a most fascinating and intriguing way of guiding us and directing us to literature, music, or other works that mould us, shape us, and assist us in our growth toward the Truth. As I wrote this chapter, and more precisely right after I wrote the prior paragraph, I had a phenomenal experience that strummed my heartstrings at my place of employment. Coincidence, I think not! I was meeting with a local roofing contractor to review some concerns with the roof of our building and was introduced to a senior company representative and a younger assistant. The three of us spoke for a few minutes prior to going to the problematic areas on the roof, and the young man was beaming with zest and enthusiasm, which was a little different for a 24-year-old at eight o'clock in the morning! He had a spring in his step and a light in his eyes that radiated understanding, and when his senior co-worker brought forth the fact that Joseph was also a musician and songwriter, I shared with them that I wrote as well and was currently writing a book.

I was compelled to share a poem or two with the two gentlemen, and Joseph relayed that he too had a poem to share with me. As I read Joseph's writing, my heartstrings were strummed immensely, and awareness was substantiated yet again by the words brought through him to paper. The poem is as follows

How can you grow into a flower if you're always being reminded of the dirt and shit you came from? Even when we're planted so close to the tree the colours look so much more vibrant when kept out of the shade. But when dark clouds form, do flowers fear what is coming or do they embrace water trickling down their petals? Do they realize at first that the change helps them grow? And when they are done and they may understand when they have fully found out their purpose, they do not stand straight above the others, they do not lower in defeat that they have accepted their possible end of the journey, they bow to the elements that gave them life. (Joseph Barras.)

Wow! This young man has awareness beyond his years, and I am so very grateful that he was put in my path to share his writing and enthusiasm toward truth! One by one, as our awareness evolves toward truth, the changes in ourselves create the changes in our world. Thanks forever, Joseph, you are indeed a light for our world!

Life perpetually introduces us to music, writings, art, and other works that tap into our truth, and when we experience these moments with an open mind and heart, the strings of the heart can indeed be touched and we can know peace at its very essence, peace that can indeed passeth all understanding! We can experience the call home through the artistic gifts bestowed upon those before us and those among us.

As we can be touched on our heartstrings during certain life events, by a special song, or intriguing book or piece of art, we can be touched on our heartstrings at will, through being still, being present in the current moment, with an absence of incessant thought. This is a place where we can experience silence within, whereby focus on any particular situation or event is as sharp as a razor. With focus on what is happening in any particular moment and without the continual chatter of the mind, we can have "Aha!" moments on a regular basis. We can witness first-hand the miracles and synchronistic events that happen each and every day and know truth at our core; we can know Love.

As I was growing up and throughout my life, it was typical to hear someone say to another that he or she couldn't walk and chew gum at the same time, typically in reference to a person's ability to focus on more than one thing at a time. This saying has been around for years and is one that most people would definitely feel offended upon hearing. Today, I believe it is imperative that we work toward acting, thinking, and living in this manner, as focus should always be directed to one task at hand. Putting heart, soul, and mental focus on what is directly in front of us within the current moment is our key to experiencing life at its fullest and our key to heartfelt moments that aid in our evolution on the ladder of life.

Yes, in this day and age, we have to multitask at work and in our home life more than ever, many times going from one thing to another on a regular basis. Cooking a gourmet meal involves a lot of activity occurring in a short span of time—preparing several components of the meal simultaneously and having the final product arrive from the cooking medium to the table at the exact time and temperature. Leisurely completing one task prior to tackling the next is not an option in situations such as this; we must plunge into the depths of many tasks at once or eliminate the magic and marvel of the finished product.

Yes, we indeed have to multitask, but when we can break down each component of that which we are doing into what one might call micro steps, with focus in each instant on exactly that which is being done, we are in fact doing one thing at a time! Doing one thing at a time and being able to put 100 percent focus on the current moment, with other activity lying just outside the boundaries of our attention, is paramount to experiencing life in ways to which we are for the most part unaccustomed. We enter what one might call "the zone," and in this zone, invigoration, inspiration, and a sense of aliveness encapsulates being, and we can feel life at our very core. It is a feeling that many chase through activities, such as vehicular racing or other activities and events that force us into this zone. Sometimes it puts us at great risk should we not focus intently on the task at hand. It provides huge risk but huge reward!

When forced into the depths of the current moment, experiencing and maintaining the task at hand is of necessity and happens for the most part naturally, without effort on anyone's part. But when we are involved in our everyday activities, staying present in the moment, staying focused on the exact task at hand is challenging, to say the least. Our thoughts tend to wander during any activity we undertake, including our everyday communication with others in our home life, social life, and work life. When our thoughts stray from words and emotions at any given time while interacting with others, we are extremely susceptible to missing the importance or the relevance of the words, expressions, and thoughts conveyed. We eliminate, or at the very least reduce, our ability to experience a heartfelt moment and time standing still. We remove ourselves from the place in which life can tap us on the shoulder and remind us of our divine existence and the divine existences of those with whom we are interacting in that precise time and space.

Our challenge in varying states of awareness and understanding is quite simply to focus on the conversations at hand and put full attention on that which we are undertaking. I say it quite simply, but in reality, it is not simple at all; in fact, it is quite the opposite. Our egos continually fight to bring us to the forefront and continually strive to stay one step ahead and one peg above those with whom we are interacting. In order to accomplish this, our ego forces our minds and our thoughts to jump forward, backward, and all around, thereby making it virtually impossible to be or remain internally silent.

Just as our thoughts jump and bounce around within conversations or even within ourselves when we are not interacting with others, we can feel the same unease in other activities, tasks, or experiences. We may be working on a project at work or at home or simply be taking a walk after dinner to unwind and work off a meal recently consumed. With full intent to do that which we plan to undertake, we many times find ourselves sidetracked, caught up in thoughts, daydreaming if you will. We lose focus and lose our ability to accomplish or fully enjoy that which we set out to do; we lose the moment. And when we lose the moment, we lose our opportunity to live life as intended—in the here and now!

When we continually deny ourselves the experience of the here and now, we deny ourselves the ability to understand that which is around us, those around us, and ourselves! We are held hostage in thought and continually attempt to figure things out and stay one step ahead, all the while trapped within the confines of our egos, whereby stillness within continually evades us. When we can finally crack the shell of incessant thought, we can begin to know the premise of the words of another phenomenal band, which I have had the pleasure and blessing to see live, the Eagles. The Eagles convey their own message of the importance of this undertaking in their song "Learn to Be Still." I particularly love the line in the song that states the world is awaiting our awakening and that we someday will, by learning to be still.

Though the world is torn and shaken
Even if your heart is breakin'
It's waiting for you to awaken
And some day you will-
Learn to be still[13]

---

[13] Written by Don Henley, Stanley Lynch • Copyright © Warner/Chappell Music, Inc, Cass County Music / Wisteria Music / Privet Music, Hori Pro Entertainment Group

Yes, each and every one of us awakens to a new reality, a new rung of understanding and awareness at some point in our existence. This is our life's purpose, be it known or not!

What allows us to stay in the moment and allows us the ability to enjoy that which we are experiencing in either activity or conversation? Internal silence, internal stillness. And how do we accomplish this to any degree of success, so that we can experience that set before us in an uninterrupted state? We recognize the awareness within and then begin to recognize the mental chatter that continually robs us of the opportunities to know ourselves in stillness itself. We strive toward catching ourselves in the confines of incessant thought, and over time, we experience a reduction in this debilitating mental chatter. With each new level of awareness, with each new level of incessant thought reduction, we build upon our abilities to be still and increase our opportunities to be touched on the strings of the heart. We allow ourselves to reach up and climb the next rung on the ladder of our existence and experience a new level of understanding that eludes us when we are void of silence within. We continually, lovingly, and gratefully evolve in our understanding of the great, the glorious, the awe-inspiring "I Am"!

Chapter 10

I AM

I Am

I Am the wind, caressing the leaves among the trees.

I Am the trees, reaching up to touch the stars.

I Am the stars, floating softly amid nothingness.

I Am.

I Am the rain, peacefully descending atop green grass and lush plants.

I Am the plants, continually emanating the source of all breath.

I Am the breath, flowing inward and outward over universal lips.

I Am.

I Am the sun, encompassing in warmth each crystal of sand.

I Am the sand, converging with heat in the form of mirage.

I Am the mirage, the illusion to all eyes that fall upon.

I Am.

I Am the river, trickling gently over rock and through soil.

I Am the soil, the womb from which sprouts the sustenance of life.

I Am Life, spontaneously given to the eternal everything.

I Am.

Awareness of life, of ourselves, and of each other is what every experience, in each facet of our lives imminently reveals. The curtain of illusion is lovingly lifted, the sleep gently swept from the corners of our eyes, and the essence of life itself gracefully infused into each beat of our heart and every breath drawn within. Understanding of the great "I Am" no longer eludes us and no longer holds us in the hands of separation. The realm of illusion, the conditioning from those who came before us, graciously falls by the wayside. We know who we are and know our part within the great "I Am."

This poem was quite different in style and structure than the others that found their way to paper – but flowed as intended through the realm of spirit, the realm of life unseen. And just as the Spirit and life flow through and are part of each component within the poem, the Spirit and life flow through us as humans as well. You see, we are part of the great "I Am," each and every one of us, and we need each other more than we could ever fathom. We are all an intricate part of the universal body, each with a distinct role and purpose—much like a human body or body of any other living being. In our bodies, billions of cells work and exist throughout, each part of a specific organ or system, with a specific function, whereby each knows not what the other cells are doing in other areas of the body. But miraculously, all come together in unison to perform their own specific function, to create us as a whole, allowing us to breathe, walk, and talk, allowing us to live!

Within any living body, the many components, parts, and systems need to contribute in one way, shape, or form. Within any living body, individual cells exist and amalgamate with others to form distinct parts or systems collectively. Within any living body, collective parts or systems work with others to make the living body and to allow the body to function as intended. Our earth, our universe, is a living body, and we are the cells that need to realize our part in its whole, in its continued existence. Individually we are parts of many collective groups, whether it be an organization, a religion, or perhaps a race. And we need to realize our individual and collective positions within our existence. We need only focus on this simple yet ever so complex point to begin to realize how much we really do need one another. Continuity of separation holds us in the realm of darkness and keeps the chains of pain wrapped tightly around our wrists, and prisoners within our own minds.

In their wonderful work "Closer to the Heart," Rush outlines the importance of each of us in our quest for a new reality. They sing of the men in high places, philosophers, plowmen, and others—all with a place and purpose in the grand scheme of things. It's a fantastic piece and an inspiration to all to do our very best in our part of the whole. As the band conveys in their message, we are moving toward our destiny, closer to the heart.

And the men who hold high places

Must be the ones who start

To mold a new reality

Closer to the heart

You can be the captain

I will draw the chart

Sailing into destiny

Closer to the heart [14]

This is our destiny. This is our purpose for which we are born in the flesh. This is our part in the great "I Am." And just as the plants need both the rain and the soil to exist and evolve, and just as we humans need the sun and the river for our own existence and evolution, we need each other as well, as part of the Whole. Coming to this realization, feeling this realization at the core of our being, is discovering the fountain of youth, and the pot of gold at the end of the rainbow! And this discovery, the greatest discovery we can ever make, evolves with the combination of our cumulative experiences and the grace of the Universe itself. Mark Twain put it so well with his short quote,

> "The two most important days of your life are the day you were born and the day you find out why."

Our current and past state of affairs has us divided into groups, organizations, classes, nationalities, religions, and every other faction

---

[14] Music- Geddy Lee and Alex Lifeson Lyrics- Neal Peart and Peter Talbot

of division and separation one could imagine. We know we are all human and we know we all exist upon the earth body, but yet we remain in turmoil, frustration, anger, hate, and separation in each of these groups or bodies collectively and within our own families, neighbourhoods, and other small groups- individually. We do not know our part in the Whole when we do not know who we are within. And when we do not know who we are within, our awareness of our part in the great "I Am" evades us and the illusion of individualism and separation continues to hold us captive within our minds and our egos, captive from freedom, and captive from Truth.

The Truth is that which we are all seeking, which we are all evolving toward, and which we are all discovering one experience at a time. And the truth is -whether we have swept the sleep from our eyes or not, or whether we have awakened to a new Reality or not, that we are all an intricate part in our evolution as a whole, as we are all teaching and we are all learning. We are all playing our part as both teachers and students at different points in our lives and our existences. With lack of understanding and awareness, we are the pupils of life, students in the flesh of existence. With varying degrees of understanding, awareness, and grace from the universe itself, we become teachers toward a new Reality, toward Unity. But these roles are often reversed, in the sense that those with some awareness and understanding can be the pupils to those without. They can observe and understand the actions, thoughts, or words of others and learn what they do not want to become or what they do not want to be. They then, in a sense, become the learner, and those lacking awareness become the teacher. So in fact, we are all learners and we are all teachers throughout our time in the flesh.

"We are continually learning and teaching, regardless of where our understanding lies in Natural law. When aligned with it, we are teachers of compassion, love, and unity, and we are learners of tolerance, open-mindedness, and understanding. When not aligned with it, we are learners of compassion, love, and unity and we are teachers of tolerance, open-mindedness, and understanding. Our human experience involves fluctuation between both."

When we know we are part in the great "I Am," we recognize and understand that the conditioning we were subjected to in our youth was of good intent and taught by those with the understanding that they themselves possessed at any specific point in time. The ways of the material world are the focal point for the most part in the teaching and conditioning of youth, with the teachers attempting to prepare and condition us for the reality that they themselves were taught and they themselves experienced. Many times, that reality is encapsulated with fears, with competition, and with separation from the great "I Am," and it is imperative to dissolve and to shed this conditioning.

Our greatest mystery as a species is that of an individual nature and is that of ourselves. As each and every one of us journeys through our life, one experience at a time, this great mystery unfolds, refolds, goes sideways, flips upside down, and spins all around, revealing our true identity each step of the way. We peel away the layers of illusion, discover the untruths, and awaken to the giant that resides within us all. That giant, that mystical, phenomenal power, is our own awareness of our part of the great "I Am." And with any living entity, whether it be a tree, an insect, or a human being, each part of that living entity, each organ or system, plays a vital role in the life of that entity. As part of our universe, that is how important each and every one of us is in its existence!

The world does not work without any of us. Each and every living being, each and every spirit, past and present, plays a vital role in the Universal Body and is contributing in some way, shape, or form to its existence and evolution. We need each other more than we could ever know, and as we hurt one another individually or collectively, we are hurting ourselves. We are only as strong as the weakest link in our chain, and we are prolonging our own suffering, again both collectively and individually-when we knowingly or unknowingly deny our unity. When we lack the awareness of this marvelous phenomenon of our Unity, we perpetuate the hurt, the confusion, and the conflict that is experienced over and over again upon our earth.

We have governments, countries, groups, organizations, and the like professing the movement and the intent to help one another, but in many cases, the intent is categorically working toward helping themselves. At the end of the day, it is not until we collectively move toward looking after the interests of *everything* and *everyone* that we will gain any real ground. In a movie I recently watched *Evan Almighty*, Steve Carell asks God, played by Morgan Freeman, the following question: "How can we go about changing the world?" God answers, "By one random act of kindness at a time."

One random act of kindness at a time, one kind word, a genuine, heartfelt concern for another, for a group, or for a country is how we will change the world, both individually and collectively. And when we know our part of the Whole, speaking, acting, and living in a fashion conducive to the greater good becomes a way of life for us, as we are now aware of our part. As eternal beings, we are either contributing to our evolution of all knowing their part of the Whole, or actively holding all of us in conflict, confusion, and ultimately separation.

Again, our greatest mystery is that of ourselves and our true identity, and again in the realm of the universe it is exactly as it is supposed to be! There are no mistakes, no errors, and nothing happening that ultimately impacts any of us as eternal beings. We are cut from the cloth of God himself, we are part of His spirit, we are His light, and we are Love! We only need to push forward one experience at a time and become aware of the great "I Am" that resides at the core of our soul.

We cannot hide, run, or escape the evolution of self-discovery; it is our mystery, and it is why we are here. Yes, we ourselves participate in unkind acts, violence, and ill will toward others at some point in our lives, but it is the atrocities that we experience or hear of in the world we live in that drive the wedge of separation deep into the heart of our being. It is the slaughter of animals, nature, and other human beings that boils the blood within and reassures us that we are not like them, we are not capable of these atrocities, and we are better. Yes, it is extremely difficult to feel any compassion or understanding toward any individual or collective body that participates in acts such as these, but as each of us has our own path to knowing Self, sometimes that path leads us down roads where murder, mayhem, and atrocities are a part of that discovery, whether it be in this lifetime or another. We need to remember eternity is a long time; eternity is forever! We do not remember all we have participated in or done in our own eternal past, and we all have the capacity of the worst sinner or the greatest saint; it is this we must come to realize to open our hearts toward understanding the actions and the atrocities of others.

When our hearts begin to blossom, when we are bestowed with the grace of awareness, and when we awaken to a new Reality upon the ladder, we can understand that the words, the actions, and the illusive atrocities have occurred by those still unaware of their own part in the great "I Am." And through our own spiritual evolution, we know that one would not and could not speak or act in such a manner if knowledge of one's true Self was not evading one; it is simply an impossibility in the grand scheme of things. Each and every one of us now and throughout eternity does the absolute best that we can with the current understanding and awareness we possess. This includes the conditioning and teaching we receive from those who have come before us, we ourselves in this current time and space, and those who will follow. It is the circle of life that we are continually changing, continually evolving toward improving by continually discovering our true Selves- one experience at a time! And as we receive the grace of awareness to better understand ourselves and therefore everyone and everything else, the grace of forgiveness aligns parallel to that grace of awareness.

Forgiveness is a word and the action that is imperative in our climb to each successive rung upon the ladder of life. Without it, we fester in failure, stew in self-loathing, and remain frustrated in our feelings toward ourselves and others. We are held captive and remain in the custody of confusion, not really ever knowing or being certain that the key is held within our own hand, our own heart. And for us to arrive at this certainty, we have the intrinsic need to really understand, really comprehend, and truly believe in the fact that we are eternal. When we can feel our eternity at our core, we know that, yes, we will do and say things that are not conducive to love and we will act in a manner that may hurt the feelings of those around us, those we love, but we also know at our core that we are forgiven in each moment in time by the Universe itself and in the next moment, the next situation, we will be given another opportunity to do or say the right thing.

This brings to memory a fantastic 1993 movie called *Groundhog Day*, starring Bill Murray and Andie McDowell. The premise of the movie was Bill Murray's character seeking the attention and love of a beautiful woman, and ultimately his discovery that he has a chance to start fresh each new day to win the heart of this beautiful woman. As he comes to the awareness of his plight and the awareness of his shortcomings through the reactions of Andie McDowell's character, he changes his approach each and every new day, learning from the mistakes of the days gone by. And with each new day, he moves closer and closer to winning the heart of the woman of his dreams, until the magical day that love arrives and he wins the heart of this woman.

We are much the same as Bill Murray's character in this movie, only we are moving toward knowing Love in the ultimate sense—knowing love through knowing Self and therefore knowing all others, knowing the great "I Am." And just as Bill Murray's character was forgiven each day for the blunders of the days past, we are forgiven each moment in time, given a new opportunity to do and say the right things, to act and speak out of compassion and understanding to all those we interact with. We are given a new opportunity to open the doors to awareness and the secrets of our soul!

When we can know the real miracle of time, that time does not really exist, forgiveness of our own words and actions and those of others then becomes possible. It not only becomes possible; it becomes our salvation from the persecution we cast upon ourselves and alleviates the guilt within for not measuring up to our own expectations and those of others. Forgiveness is the key that unlocks the chains of time and the chains of confusion; we need only place the key into our hearts to release ourselves and all those around us. When we can place the key and the key is lovingly turned by the grace of Love, forgiveness is the gift we receive to move forward in our evolution and therefore move the great "I Am" forward in its own evolution. One heart at a time, the great "I Am" is changing the world!

The day arrives for us all to come to the deep realization of our part in the Whole, and to know our part in the great "I Am". There is no question as to our arrival, only a question of what point in time each of us arrives. We are all awakening through our lives, through our experiences, and thus learning our true nature. We are coming into the realization of our part in the Whole and coming to the realization of our own importance in the grand scheme of things.

This importance is much different than we typically experience; it is an importance encapsulated in humility and saturated in gratitude, an importance that no position, material gain, or stroke of our ego could ever come close to. Coming face to face with our part in the great "I Am" brings us to the realization that deep down, at our core "I Am"! This is why we are here, this is why we experience all that we do, and this is the greatest gift that one could ever receive—the gift of awareness.

Chapter 11

THE GIFT

The Gift

Today I awoke for the first time in my life,

My thoughts were not cluttered with anger or strife.

Sometime in the night, the Gift touched my Being,

The Gift changed my eyes and the way they'd been seeing.

My eyes had seen things, and my mind had believed,

But the Gift reassured me that I'd been deceived.

Judgment of all did gracefully slip away

As the Gift bestowed Unity upon awakening this day.

The world as we know it is a journey for mankind,

For all, in time, the Gift they will find.

Once found all that is will fall into place,

For we are all connected throughout time, throughout space.

One day will come when I return to my start,

And the Gift will be there in full spirit and heart.

Until that time, I will journey with Love,

The Gift shall help me from heaven above.

From heaven above and from deep within,

The Gift unfolds my destiny and places I've been.

The Gift lives in all of us, waiting to reveal-

Not our reality, but that which is Real.

The gift was the first poem that I wrote, or that came to my awareness, back in September of 2007. Through some personal trials at this point in my life, I found myself peering into the mirror of my existence with deep questions and an honest longing for understanding. A longing to know the questions that I had spoken of earlier: Who am I? Where did I come from? And why am I here? It is a longing that we all possess, be it known to us or not. I had been reading and reflecting on some spiritually based and spiritually inspired books, and suddenly, very uncharacteristically, I began to write the poem "The Gift." I had never really written any poetry before in my life; it was probably one of the least likely things that I would see myself having any interest in and actually undertaking. My life to this point was focused on my family, my career, and some sporting activities—writing poetry? No way!

When the idea, the awareness, first entered my consciousness, I immediately experienced a motivation and inspiration unlike anything I had encountered before. It was pushing me, challenging me to write and complete this poem. This was unique to any other challenge in my life to this point, as a spark within quickly transformed into a flame. This challenge was one that I embraced with an enthusiasm that I had long forgotten existed or was possible. Upon reflection, this experience was another very intense and distinctive moment in time and space on my spiritual journey toward knowing Self. I completed this poem within a day or so, the first two verses almost immediately upon awareness of the task put before me. "Of Time and Oneself" came a couple of weeks later, and then nine more poems were put to paper between September 2007 and early January 2009.

At the time that these poems came to fruition, I could not believe that I had written them, and could not believe the feelings that they stirred within while I was writing and upon completion. After several years, I now realize where these poems originated and know it was not I or my mind that created and wrote this poetry. Yes, it was a part of me that I have come to know to be of utmost importance, the only segment bearing any reality, the part that resides within me and within us all, the element that lovingly binds us to everyone and everything—the Universal Heart, the Universal Mind.

Although I experienced an extreme sense of peace in the creation of these poems, it was not until the near past that I came to know them at my core in my Being. Upon putting the pen to paper and writing these poems, I was most definitely inspired and was granted an extreme sense of joy in their conception. I believed in the content and words contained within but remained in a state of separation, ruled by the ever incessant ego, for quite some time afterward. There were yet many experiences to encounter, many trials, tribulations, and life events to unfold before the hands of time came to a halt within. Illusory thoughts and perceptions continued to hold me in the bond of self, with short, intermittent glances of expansive awareness. Unwanted thoughts and perceptions continued to creep into my consciousness like a thief in the night, but the house I now reside in with All, has a detection system that cuts short any illusory intrusion! These poems have infiltrated my thoughts and awareness, and now lovingly hold me deep within the world I have sought to rediscover, experience, and cherish- aligned with the divine scheme of things.

Throughout our lives, gifts are given, received, loved, hated, appreciated, despised, regarded, or ignored. We typically think of gifts as that which is given or received at celebratory moments, such as birthdays, weddings, and the like. Receiving gifts as child can be such an amazing experience- the anticipation, the happiness and pleasure tearing into the Christmas presents preciously placed under the tree by the jovial chap in red. As we mature and have children of our own, we relive the anticipation and excitement as they follow in our situational footsteps, many times experiencing a true moment of joy when seeing the twinkle in their eyes, and the ear to ear smile impressed upon their face!

As time shifts forward, material gifts become a way of life, a social prerequisite, and most definitely a huge cog in the wheels of retail profit, and our economy. We all experience the conversations and grumblings of the commercialism of holidays and other moments of relevance, and yet year after year many continue to acquire cumulative debt, or spend too much despite the words we have spoken to ourselves, or others. There is absolutely nothing wrong with giving, and receiving material or monetary gifts, but societal norms have elevated us to a point of collective craziness! We are missing the mark of spiritual growth, when emphasise continually shines on materialism, gifts from others, or gifts or financial rewards bestowed by life itself.

The material gifts that we receive in life are often appreciated by the recipient, something sentimental can indeed be cherished for a lifetime. But most gifts become yesterday's news, appreciated for the most part, but quickly forgotten. The greatest gifts we can ever really receive are not material whatsoever, but those of a spiritual nature. In my experience, two of the greatest gifts that can be received come to light- awareness and understanding. We all have varying degrees of these gifts within our possession at any given point in time, and upon any rung of the ladder. It is the moment in clock time, and upon the rung of the ladder of life when we recognize that these indeed are the greatest gifts we can receive. The moment in time, when time ceases to exist– and we feel our immortality at our core, and gloriously frolic in the fountain of youth. The moment in time we recognize our true Selves. No amount of money, material possessions, or social, political, or any other status symbols can come close to the realization of who we really are!

Every experience we encounter throughout our lives leads to this point, to the rung of the ladder of awareness and understanding of our part in the Whole, our completeness. And again, as eternal beings, this point in clock time varies from person to person, soul to soul. We awaken to this awareness and understanding in our own time, in our own experiences, and in our own way. There is one final component of our awakening in which we have no part, that being the grace of God or whatever else one might recognize, ultimately the grace of the Universe itself. There are as many paths to reaching this rung of awareness and understanding as there are feet walking upon the earth, as no two paths are the same.

No two paths are the same in our journey, but in our awakening, we land on a common path upon which we now tread. That common path is one in which our thoughts, actions, and presence experience sheer joy touching the heartstrings of another, as we now recognize ourselves in every other. We share a moment when we both recognize at our core our Divine heritage. Literally ten minutes ago, as I was writing this chapter, this occurred for me, as I had a wonderful encounter with a local woman named Gina, whom I recognized from conversations in the past, in a local coffee shop where I have done a lot of my writing.

She had no previous knowledge of my writing but often saw me in my writing spot on her way to work in the mornings, always offering a smile and saying "Good Morning." She may have assumed I was working, and today, a Sunday, she inquired as to whether I was working. I proceeded to tell her I was not working but writing a book. She immediately asked if I was writing a novel, and I felt compelled to share I was writing a book of a spiritual nature. Her demeanour immediately indicated her interest, and I began to explain that the book came about as an idea several months earlier, one morning in March of 2015. I went on to tell her that I had written several poems years earlier, and on this day, this idea, this inspiration- then outlined the poems I had written would form the chapters of the book. I proceeded to read her a paragraph I had just written, as well as a few of the poems, and we both experienced a moment that was inspirational and memorable indeed. We both recognized the truth in the writing, and after she left, upon reflection, my spirit was unmistakably touched, as the hairs on my body were elevated to a glorious degree. She thanked me several times for starting her day in such an enjoyable manner and offered me encouragement and inspiration for the completion of the book. Wow, this was an amazing experience, a gift on which one could never put a price tag!

Touching the realm of Spirit within another is paramount in our newfound rung of awareness, as our journey shifts from individual wants and desires to the wants and desires of *all*. And upon the awareness and understanding of our unity, upon knowing our importance in the Whole of life itself, we now move in whatever direction life takes us to touch the heartstrings of others. We now utilize the God-given gifts and talents we possess to assist in the awakening and awareness in all others. As outlined in an earlier chapter, this can be in the creation of art, music, or literature, or it can be in our career path, a group we join, a cause we stand behind, or any other form of expression. At the end of it all, our true heart's desire is to experience others experiencing that which we have now come to understand ourselves—the sheer joy of knowing our true Selves and knowing our connection. This is the gift of awareness and understanding; this is the gift of Truth.

The gift of truth is revealed to all of us not by learning but ultimately by unlearning, by peeling away the layers of illusion as outlined in chapter 2. As illusory thoughts, ideas, and ways of life are passed from generation to generation, as we are conditioned by those who came before us, much of that learned ultimately must be shed. There are, of course, those who come before us in families, groups, or other influential bodies who possess the gift of truth, but this is the extreme exception, definitely not the rule. As well as external conditioning we absorb from others, we evolve ourselves in our early years with many of our own thoughts and ideas from our own eternal past. Those thoughts and ideas that ultimately hold us in the realm of separation and individuality, and many times compound to the point of extreme confusion - but ultimately lead us to ask ourselves who we really are. Thoughts and ideas that require transcendence through the illusion they create. When we transcend our illusory self and recognize our true nature at our core, we can feel, breathe, and know the truth. Persian poet Rumi said it so well in his work "In Baghdad, Dreaming of Cairo: In Cairo Dreaming of Baghdad." The following is taken from the book *The Essential Rumi*, from the last few lines of the poem:

> So it came quietly to the seeker, though he didn't say it loud,
> "What I'm longing for lived in my house in Baghdad!"
> He filled with joy. He breathed continuous praise.
> Finally he said, "The water of life is here. I'm drinking it. But
> I had to come this long way to know it!"

Climbing the rungs upon our ladder of life is most definitely a long process of peeling away the many layers of illusion, one experience at a time. It's a long way to knowing our truth and thus the truth of all others, a long way to knowing that categorizing, judging, analysing, labelling, or thinking of anyone or anything in one distinct manner or another is not aligned with truth. When we have shed the final layers of our illusion, we are no longer aligned with steadfast opinions on anything and we accept the multitude of situations and experiences of life itself and know there really is no right or wrong; *there just is!*

We may not agree with, endorse, or support any specific situation, experience, or behaviour in relation to ourselves or others, but deep down, we know and accept that every situation and experience evolves exactly as it should to bring all of us to know the truth. Individual and collective experiences and events are occurring in a synchronistic manner, which ultimately brings us all to truth's door.

Today several friends and I who grew up together have to face a truth that is often very hard for anyone to comprehend, very hard to accept or understand. We are going to a funeral visitation tonight, as a friend we grew up with for the good part of our high school years took his own life just over a week ago. He left behind a seven-year-old son, who will likely face some hardships of his own as a direct result. It is often common to hear people question how anyone could commit such an act upon him- or herself and the loved ones who are left behind. Many comment on the selfishness of this undertaking, whereby the real pain is left behind to be experienced by those left in the wake. There may be truth in this line of thought, and there is no doubt that those left behind often experience the repercussions of the situation. But the truth is everyone does the utmost best that they can at any moment of time, with the understanding and awareness they possess.

As there are as many paths to truth as there are people walking the face of the earth, we can really only know the feelings and the state of understanding when they are our own. There is a saying that we mustn't judge a person until we walk a thousand miles in his or her shoes, and it is this we must remember in times such as this. We all make decisions or partake in actions in our lives that we ourselves and others do not understand. It is this which we must remember and reflect upon in times such as this. Rest in peace, Darrin.

The gift of awareness and understanding touches all of us in an individual manner, but ultimately, with commonality, it directs us to the truth. Today, November 11, we commemorate and honour the men and women who gave their lives in battle for our freedom, who fought for the collective bodies they were a part of. Yes, there is no doubt that freedom was gained in many ways, shapes, and forms as a result, but in reality, it is freedom gained at the cost of human lives, with the annihilation of others and ultimately ourselves. It is freedom that perpetuates the insane human condition that has existed and continues to exist.

As we move forward as a species in our spiritual evolution, we are recognizing the truth, recognizing the gift of our true Selves, one experience and one soul at a time. I believe that there will come a point in clock time when we may recognize another Remembrance Day, a day we reflect upon our remembering of who we really are, remember our gift of Unity, and remember that true freedom is only accomplished through loving, understanding words or actions and never through anything else, individually or collectively.

Another gift that we can receive upon the ladder that is introduced to our awareness is that of embracing life and all of its seen and unseen circumstances and experiences, embracing, or accepting if you will, all the moments, whether deemed good or bad, right or wrong, fair or unfair. Most of us naturally and easily embrace the moments of success, victory, happiness, and comfort. On the flip side, few of us naturally or easily embrace the moments that throw us into a state of hurt, shame, fear, or concern. Most certainly, circumstances and experiences arise that weigh horrendously heavily upon our hearts and upon our spirits. Experiences that often place us upon rungs of despair and have us questioning ourselves, others, and the reality of any Divine presence.

These experiences occur for many and often occur frequently. Very often, some type of resolution arrives to calm circumstantial or experiential waves of turmoil, only to have others take form and hold us in their grasp. And all too often, they can hold us in their grasp until they crash upon the shores of perpetual anguish, and we drearily wait upon the shore for the arrival of the next. We can become tattered and torn, tired and worn, whereby we exist upon the plane of simple existence in hurt, confusion, and an overall sense of malaise. We feel life continually give us a one-two punch, and we find it harder and harder to get up off the mat, harder and harder to stick our chin forward for the next bout. We cannot embrace or accept anything coming our way, as we now feel life is beating us to a pulp. And when in this corner of the ring, we will continually be beaten to a pulp, until we have experienced enough inner pain and anguish to move us to a different rung of understanding—or in this case, a different ring of understanding!

There comes a moment in time upon the ladder when we do recognize the importance and reality of embracing and accepting all circumstances and experiences exactly for what they are—circumstances and experiences! We obviously may not care for or like that which we face, but a sense of Higher purpose remains gently within our consciousness, a sense that keeps us upon a solid rung of awareness and understanding. Inclusive to these circumstances or experiences are those void of any real consciousness as they occur, circumstances or experiences that do toss us into a state of turmoil in the midst of their arrival and throughout various durations of their existence. We may experience varying degrees of confusion or upset as they occur, but reflection and acceptance are a short distance behind, often with further understanding and a firmer grip upon our rung of awareness. These experiences no longer hold us in the grip of psychological time, continually playing the tape over and over, continually holding us hostage within our own minds. Life still happens and circumstances and events still occur that activate our internal fight-or-flight instinct, but now we have a different awareness and understanding that we must accept whatever hand is dealt at any moment in time.

By not holding the events and circumstances in the grip of psychological time, we disallow ourselves the opportunity to play victim to whatever experiences we encounter. We embrace the reality that whatever comes our way is only meant to water our leaves of spiritual growth and to move us a little closer to knowing and understanding unconditional Love. And by not playing victim to all of the circumstances, events, and experiences we encounter in day-to-day life, we prevent our identity from accumulating residual hurt, pain, fear, and resentment. By embracing, by accepting all that crosses our path in our day-to-day life, we have planted our existence on the rung of understanding that all that comes our way is ultimately required. All that comes our way brings us step by step, experience by experience, toward our real identity among the most fascinating race.

When we arrive upon the rung of unity through the gift of Grace, we can really know that we are a part of the most fascinating race, a race that most perplexingly holds all of us for varying amounts of time so that we believe that there must always be winners and always be losers in the game of life. It is a race that physically, psychologically, and emotionally places us in every type of competition imaginable in which we ultimately absorb a check in either the win or loss column. It is a race that ultimately declares both victories and losses for all, as no single individual can receive the victory ribbon in every event, circumstance, or experience.

We are all naturally ingrained to varying degrees with the will to win, with the drive to survive, and we often hear that we live in a world of "survival of the fittest." We are also conditioned from early in life as to what the picture of victory looks like, what deems us a winner or loser in the game of life, and what separates the men from the boys. Most certainly our experiences with competition can be positive in our growth and overall sense of esteem, as we have seen in Maslow's hierarchy of needs (Physiological; safety; love/belonging; esteem; self-actualization; self-transcendence). We most definitely need to arrive at a place where our needs are met, and we should definitely take pride in the perseverance required to compete in a sporting event or any other event in which we strive for our personal best. This is what we have come to know as "healthy competition," competition that drives us beyond illusory limits that we often place upon ourselves.

Ultimately, this type of competition is a miniscule part of what we experience on a regular, frequent basis. The competitions that occur incessantly on a regular basis are those that either inflate or deflate our egos subconsciously. They present themselves in our everyday lives, everyday experiences, and everyday interactions and conversations with others, and perpetually rank us in our own illusory standings-and those of others. These ongoing subconscious competitions occur in the family home, the workplace, the boardroom, city hall, and everywhere else in our material world.

When we can wholeheartedly shed the illusion that to win or lose invariably controls the way that we feel about ourselves, we can know the gift of our spirit. We can come to know that in the game that we call life, there really are no winners or losers, only divine participants, watching and experiencing the great game unfolding. We develop a new sense or desire to take on more of a coaching role, to feel the love and glory within when we can wave a team member past third base, so he or she too may find his or her way to home plate. Ultimately we are not here to compete or to place the worth of others or ourselves on any circumstance, event, or situation. We are here to know our own part in humanity and the universe and that we are in fact part of the most fascinating race.

Ultimately, the journey to the awareness that we do indeed exist in the most fascinating race evades arrival until such time that we enter and play the game of life in a multitude of circumstances and experiences. And ultimately, it is the circumstances and experiences that we encounter that find us challenging our source of resolve and our source of answers—both externally and from within the confines of our own minds. When answers inevitably fall by the wayside and we are left in the void of illusion, we can know that the proverbial straw has been placed upon our hearts and minds. We can experience the Source within, whereby any answer to any question ever asked can be revealed.

Often, the proverbial straw is placed upon us in a circumstance or experience that can feel horrendously overwhelming at the time. We may see ourselves hanging on the edge of our own understanding and be in a time of great emotional pain. This is a time when we can experience a miraculous crack in our incessant ego. From within this glorious crack exudes our true Selves, and the discovery of our Unity in the most fascinating race! It is a time when we see the world through an unconventional set of eyes and understand at our core that all the experiences, trials, tribulations, and circumstances within our lives occurred exactly as needed to bring us to this new point in time. One cannot really explain this time in words but really only know it within. Ultimately, we can thank the universe for every experience we ever encountered, both good and bad.

It is the proverbial straw that can break the camel's back and bring us to a new point in awareness and understanding, but it is the multitude of straws, the multitude of experiences that we encounter throughout our lives that bring us to the point of the last straw being placed upon us. They are the straws of life each of us face day in and day out as we mature in our spiritual journey. Each straw of adversity, each straw of victory, each straw of confusion, ultimately each straw of experience stacks upon us and peels away the layers of illusion in which we are all encased. These are the experiences each of us needs at the precise time to elevate us on the Eternal Ladder. We encounter them with both admiration and repulsion and deem each positive or negative, good or bad. And as eternal beings, we know not when this exact moment in time will occur, but rest assured, the time comes for us all. We cannot escape ourselves or the inherent path we all take to discover who we really are!

Upon the rung of understanding that allows us to fully accept and fully comprehend that all we encounter is of necessity, a new light shines upon each new experience. Accompanying each new experience is a subtle knowing that all will be well and even the circumstances and situations that appear hurtful, negative, or wrong ultimately lead to our understanding of Love. The straws of life we continue to experience no longer accumulate the weight they once did, as we comprehend our requirement of each new straw for additional growth. We are eternally grateful for the gift, the straw that broke the camel's back!

Upon the many rungs of life's ladder that we find ourselves upon, peering out through our own windows, our own eyes often become our gauge of accomplishment in our material world. We see what we are or what we are not. We see what we have or that which we lack. We see fear, or we see love. We look upon the mirror of life, and its reflection pushes the corners of our mouths toward the heavens or pulls them down toward illusory hell. Its reflection lights our eyes with passion and fire or blankets them with an ashen haze. And as circumstance and experience show, we often find ourselves at different points within our lives admiring or detesting the reflection that we see and the reflection that we feel.

The reflections that rebound back through our eyes and fall upon our spirit accumulate within, and are ultimately transposed into the demeanour we ourselves emanate to the world around us. We carry the weight of the world upon our shoulders, or we tread lightly with a spring of contentment in our steps. And once again, we often find ourselves fluctuating between these two states, depending on the life situation or the life experience we are encapsulated within at any specific point in time. Life has its way with each of us, and each reflection that finds its way back into our core Being accrues, only to release itself in one way or another, generating yet another reflection.

When we ultimately arrive upon the rung of life that displays our reflections in an entirely different manner, we comprehend that every reflection that we both see and feel is a requirement for further understanding and awareness. We understand the reflections that find their way back to us have no real lasting effect but serve only to open our eyes and our hearts to different stages of awakening, different stages of awareness, and different stages of Love. The reflections that burned our being and stung our soul now emanate with grace and understanding; each was a requirement to allow us to look into the mirror of Life with a different set of eyes. Eyes that now fall upon each experience, situation, and event with underlying acceptance and reflect true knowledge of who we really are when we look deep within.

We peer into the mirror of our existence time and time again, judging ourselves, others, and our world based on the reflection that falls upon our being. We experience multitudes of hurt, discontent, anger, joy, pleasure, gratitude, and malaise. Each experience directs us forward in either fear or love, and each experience ends in an elevated sense of separation or unity. And with each experience, we gravitate toward Unity, the ultimate reflection we all discover in our own space and time!

Time is the entity that wraps its hands around us and holds us all too often in its devastating grip. It often finds us stuck in our past, be it with illusions of success, failure, or anything else in between. The images, feelings, and impact of our past experiences are projected upon the screen within our minds, in both perceived victories and imagined defeats. And as the victories and defeats continue to accumulate upon our egos, they frequently derive our moods, sense of well-being, and overall state of mind.

Just as detrimental to our spiritual awareness and growth as being stuck in our past is our projection and attention to what is to come in the future. Our projection is frequently obscured by our experiences and attitudes about our past and present, either deemed good or bad, positive or negative. Periodic visions of where we want to be, who we want to become, and what we want to accomplish are not that of which I speak; it is of the incessant nature whereby we project our lives and our increased happiness and satisfaction, based on expectations, such as more money, a new love in our life, or a new job. These expectations monopolize our minds a great deal of our waking moments and impede our ability to stay in the only moment we should be living in—the present.

Whether we are stuck in our past, longing for our future, or many times an amalgamation of both, we are in the grip of psychological time. Time becomes our enemy, and we continually go to war within our minds, forever searching for victory or at least a truce. Yes, we can indeed experience worldly victories, but internally, subconsciously, we feel our mortality; we know our time in our current life, our current situation, must come to an end. Time is the greatest unknown threat to our earthly existence, to our egos.

Transcendence through psychological time becomes our Reality, when we know at our core that we are ultimately a part of eternity, a part of the Whole, a part of God. The past becomes a reflection of our growth in our awareness, and the future welcomes us to understanding yet to be revealed. An understanding that our current state moves us to the next rung upon the ladder of life. This awareness allows us to sip from the fountain of youth, and we can experience an aliveness and sense of peace, in whatever moment this gift, this grace is bestowed upon us.

The time we have come to know, come to understand, serves one purpose and one purpose only. Its purpose ultimately leads us to the realization that time really doesn't exist! We move through eternity one experience after another, one thought or reflection after another, one life, one existence after another. We move through eternity diminishing our fears, thereby growing in Love. We move through eternity discovering our Divine heritage- and that of everyone else as well. Time is no longer our enemy; it just simply *is*. Each moment, each experience finds us evolving into the next, ultimately discovering who we really are, and who we are, we only discover in time!

The gift of time ultimately knocks on the doors of our awareness and alerts us that a better way is on the other side and we need no longer tread it alone. This way finds us joined with everyone and everything else within our existence. This gift, this awareness is the universe calling, often very subtly but sometimes very loudly. Inevitably it calls each and every one of us, and in our own space and time, we begin to recognize and appreciate the miraculous phenomenon that we are experiencing. We develop an internal sense of understanding that eluded our past and now recognize we really are no different than everything else that exists in the world and in nature.

In nature, we see the universal call to wildlife, to plants and vegetation, and to our climate and atmosphere itself. We see that in the wild creatures need to perish to sustain others. We see that water is required to evaporate and then fall and sustain plants and vegetation that ultimately create the oxygen we require to breathe and to live. In our climate and atmosphere, we see the sun rise each day, the perfect distance from our planet to keep life on earth sustainable. With astounding synchronicity, the universe melds all life forms and conditions together, calling to each entity to do its part in the whole of existence. Nature doesn't question the call; nature follows that which is set out for universal evolution. There is only one species, one life form, one entity that questions and often evades the Universal call—we humans!

We as humans often fail to recognize our place in the grand scheme of things, that we are an integral part of the whole, just like the trees, water, sun, and moon. We have been given the gift of consciousness, but most often fall victim to the incessant part of us that screams for our individuality and uniqueness—our egos! Our egos continually reaffirm our separation through comparison and judgment and fool us into believing that we call the shots, we control all that occurs within our lives, and we are the captains of our own ships. In *The Big Red Book* (*Coleman Barks*), Rumi points out how much control we really have when he says, "Do you think I know what I am doing? That for one breath or half breath I belong to myself. As much as a pen knows what it is writing or the ball can guess where it is going next" (pg.378). Yes, we need direction, determination, and purpose, and no doubt these are recognized in our attitude toward life each day. But it is in the moments when we solely believe we control all of these factions of our lives that we are cast upon the seas of despair, the seas of uncertainty.

We are called upon and guided by the universe itself, just like all other living things. We are called upon and guided to know our purpose, to know our place in this amazing universe, and to know our Divine heritage. When we stray from the call, when we act, think, and carry ourselves in a manner not conducive to universal harmony, the universe either gently or aggressively calls us back to the path of discovery, the path of our own spiritual evolution. We may stumble, we may fall, and we may be temporarily broken but only to the point at which we venture one rung closer to recognition of who we really are and that all that occurs within our existence is essential in our evolution.

Our own evolution then beckons us in assisting others in their evolution, in their discovery of Self. When our evolution carries us upon the rung of understanding of our Unity, we then make every attempt to act, speak, and conduct ourselves in a manner conducive to assisting others in their recognition of their own Divinity. We see this not only in direct comments, statements, or interactions with others, but in works of art, literature, music, or any other gift bestowed upon an individual or collective group to move us all forward in awareness and understanding. The universe does call, and ultimately we all listen!

We are continually evolving, changing, and growing in understanding of ourselves, others, and the universe in which we live. We continually evolve through each moment, each experience, each lifetime to awaken to our Unity and the understanding that everything in existence is part of the whole, part of the universe, part of God. We are one with all of creation, and everything and everyone plays a critical, vital role in existence—the saints and sinners, the good and the bad, the strong and the weak, people of every skin colour and language and every other illusory component of humanity that emanates our differences both individually and collectively.

Topping any gift that we could ever receive is that of intimately knowing, intimately feeling our unity, our *Oneness*. It is a gift that once established and ingrained at our core can ease the day-to-day experiences we all encounter whereby we do not see eye to eye with another. We humbly understand that differences have and will continue to occur, as each and every one of us is climbing the ladder of life, and we are all on different rungs of awareness and understanding. We humbly understand the relevance and importance of everything and everyone around us, even when individuals or groups speak or act in a manner deemed wrong, destructive, or hateful. We internally accept that everything and everyone truly is perfect in every moment of space and time and everyone is doing the absolute best he or she can with the current understanding and awareness he or she possesses.

With awareness of our unity, we also evolve to understand the intricacies and the synchronicity of the events happening in each particular moment of space and time. We come to know that coincidences do not exist, that everything and everyone is working and moving toward the evolution of our universe, through every experience and interaction that occurs. The Universal mind, the Master computer, continually absorbs and computes what will happen next to each and every one of us individually and collectively, based on what has occurred each moment or experience prior. Every event correlates to another, and through synchronicity, we evolve each moment into the next with each evolutionary experience bringing all of us a step closer to understanding ourselves, our universe, and our oneness. When we know we are One, we really have won! We have won our position upon the eternal ladder that reassures our Divinity, through both experience and grace.

Another profound gift we encounter upon the ladder are the

experiences, the moments, the occasions in which time stands still and we are gracefully touched on our heartstrings—the moments in life whereby we experience true bliss, pure joy, and pure Love. These experiences touch that which is real in all of us, the love of God, the love of the universe contained within all of our hearts. We experience times such as these in our lives on occasions, such as when attending weddings, watching our children in a play, hearing a magically composed song, or reading words and messages in a book, to name a few. These are times when we feel an extreme sense of peace and wellness, and the only thing upon our minds during our experience is the experience itself. They lift the corners of our mouths and the hairs on our bodies toward the heavens. We often reflect upon them within our memories, trying to relive the feelings long after the experience itself.

It is these moments in time that we all subconsciously strive for, as nothing can compare to being touched on our heartstrings by life itself. No material possession, no personal victory or any other life experience comes close to bringing the true joy that falls upon us. But as everyday life happens and these experiences are often few and far between, we can actually hinder their frequency or intensity by that which is sitting upon our psyches, that which is churning within our thoughts, that which is impeding our ability to still ourselves and our minds. When we are intently committed to any situation wholeheartedly, such as life events or the experiences just spoken of, our minds become still and we are intensely focused and fully prepared to be touched by life itself, touched upon our heartstrings.

Within everyday events and experiences, we can be touched at our core in a similar way when we can recognize and appreciate the importance and the gift of stilling our minds. When we can focus on any individual occurrence or experience without any incessant mind chatter, we open ourselves to the grace of the Master musician, who lovingly strums our heartstrings, often resulting in an "Aha!" moment. But stilling ourselves can often be a challenging undertaking, evading us entirely when our minds simply refuse to cooperate. Stilling ourselves in our day-to-day activities can also pose a constant distraction, as we go through our days intensely involved in our jobs, our home life, or any other activities that swallow the hours of each day. As time marches on, in this day and age, we find ourselves multitasking more and more, continually striving to keep our heads above the water, keep one step ahead, or keep unwanted thoughts and experiences at bay with continual distractions. So how do we experience these moments of joy in our everyday lives and situations? We strive to stay in our current moment and focus on that which is set before us, and we ask for assistance in accomplishing this from life itself! When we ask for help, it will arrive with loving grace and an understanding and awareness will be present while the strings of the heart, the strings of love are strummed within. We can experience joy and bliss in the simplest of events or occurrences, as we know at our core that life is unfolding and revealing itself to us and aiding us in our continual evolution toward knowing our divinity!

Gifts bestowed upon us in our eternal journey upon the ladder of life come to each of us in our own time and the time in which the universe itself grants us the grace of understanding the relevance of the gifts themselves. Inclusive to the gifts the universe bestows upon us is our awareness and understanding of our part and the parts of all others in the great "I Am."

The awareness of the great "I Am" does not constitute any singular neatly packaged description, as it is experienced and understood by each of us in our own way. There is, however, one common seed in our awareness – our unity and the relevance and importance of each and every thing and every one of us in our universe. Without this at our core, we cannot really relate to each and every experience and interaction incurred as part of the whole, part of the universal evolution of ourselves, our brothers and sisters, and our entire existence. As described in the chapter "I Am," we are all an intricate part of the universal body, similar to the cells within our own bodies, which all play their own part in coming together and allowing us to eat, breathe, and live.

Without each and every cell contained in our systems and organs, we could not exist as human beings. Without each and every one of us, our universal body could not exist. This is how important each and every one of us truly is! With this awareness, we begin to move toward living our lives for the good of all and understanding the synchronicity of events around us, each intended to bring us closer to the heart of awareness. We develop the realization that even though life's events and experiences are not always picture perfect, many times, by far, we need each and every one for our development and growth in self-awareness and our awakening to understanding unconditional Love.

Our part in the great "I Am" fluctuates throughout our existence, along with the masks we wear and the roles we play. The stage may be set within our lives, containing themes of drama, excitement, wealth, poverty, or anything else imaginable. In eternity, our feet fall upon a multitude of stages, each one moving us toward self-awareness in one way or another, each one taking us upon the paths required to assist us on our eternal climb up the ladder of life. We play our parts upon the world's stage with each successive role lifting the curtain of awareness and opening our eyes and hearts to our own divinity and that of all others. When the curtain lifts high enough, we can then face each role with a sense of peace and understanding that everything will be all right no matter what play we partake in—for ourselves, our loved ones, and all others.

This morning, as I sit in the place the last few poems came to paper back in early 2008, I reflect upon all that I have experienced from this point and how much my thinking and awareness has changed since then. I reflect upon the radical change that occurred just about a year ago that initiated the start of writing this book. I also reflect on my gratitude for all the twists and turns I have experienced thus far in my life, now realizing the essentiality of each and every one.

Each and every one of all of our experiences, deemed good or bad, right or wrong, positive or negative, does not happen by accident; it ultimately happens for our progression and evolution upon the ladder of life, the ladder of self-awareness. Through eternity, we wear an assortment of masks, we play a variety of roles, and we partake in a multitude of situations, relationships, and events with each experience playing a pivotal, underlying role in one shape or form toward our own evolution. We see evolution all around us in technology, learning, and physical and psychological abilities to name a few, and this we cannot deny. We also see our own evolution as human beings from our youth, through adolescence, and into adulthood as our bodies, minds, abilities, and thoughts change at different stages of our existence. It is our eternal evolution that lies at the core of the poems and the core of this book and I trust will touch some who have read it. It is our evolution to knowing at our core who we really are, how important we are, and why we experience all that we do, knowing our unity, and knowing unconditional Love.

Unconditional Love, the love of God, allows each and every one of our souls and spirits to live life one experience at a time, without demands or conditions. It sets about to accept us and love us exactly as we are, absolutely, no matter what! We never return to Love and to God kicking and screaming; we return out of desire and gratitude, as we see the path to our salvation and wholeness through our return to Unity. Unity with everyone and everything else and thus with God. As the paths of untruth are tread upon countless times throughout our existence, the layers of illusion ultimately peel away one experience at a time and move us on a multitude of rungs upon the ladder of life, the ladder of truth, the ladder of Love. May we all join together and help one another to the top- where the sky truly isn't the limit!

Printed in the United States
By Bookmasters